ENTERPRISIN(

ENTERPRISING CHILD

Developing your child's entrepreneurial potential

A practical guide for parents of children
aged 4 to 14 years

Lorraine Allman
with Mary Cummings

bookshaker

First Published In Great Britain 2012
by www.BookShaker.com

© Copyright Lorraine Allman
Front cover photograph: Little Builder © Gorilla – Fotolia.com

Praise for Enterprising Child

"We live in turbulent times of change and financial upheaval. Adults rarely nowadays have just one occupation, job or single career. *Enterprising Child* is a fascinating and practical book which will support and empower you as a parent to understand the mindset and attitude necessary to teach your children the all-important skills for life in the world of work. With over a hundred structured ideas according to your child's age and plenty of inspiration along the way to help, you will have a roadmap for successfully encouraging, nurturing and understanding your child's entrepreneurial characteristics so you can feel relaxed, positive and confident in your adventure to unlock your child's true potential."

Sue Atkins, ITV *This Morning* Parenting Expert, Parent Coach,
Author of *Parenting Made Easy – How To Raise Happy Children*
and Ambassador for the Home Start charity.

"Children need ideas, an encouraging environment and a little direction to learn a creative process. *Enterprising Child* is an exceptional resource for parents, which gives practical ideas that can be used to inspire children to be free-thinking spirits in today's enterprising world. Learn how to use your environment, to nurture your child in seeking wonderful opportunities for growth and potential. Unlock the uniqueness and special talent in your child."

Priya Desai, Speech and Language Therapist, Children's Author

"*Enterprising Child* is a superb resource, not just for parents, but also for teachers wanting to understand more about entrepreneurial behaviour, skills, and attitudes. The book is well researched with activities which are not just age appropriate, but which will also support enterprising activities taking place in the classroom. With a guiding hand rather than a 'do it this way' approach, I am sure that *Enterprising Child* will be a fantastic source of inspiration and support to parents and educators wanting to help children make the best of their natural talents and abilities."

Danielle Ellis, primary school teacher

"Lorraine understands the importance and trends of entrepreneurship. To her it is a way of life. She has a strong knowledge of how to develop and establish businesses that work practically around people's circumstances and responsibilities (like childcare). She's given me great ideas for developing my own children's entrepreneurial curiosity and skills. These have always been successful and popular with my family. It's wonderful to see my children awaken at such a young age to the fact that there are opportunities to make money (and they enjoy it!). The benefit of knowing Lorraine will long ring in our lives."

Mel Maritz, Coach and Trainer, mum to Murray (4) and Aidan (1)

"If you're looking for a resource to help you understand and nurture entrepreneurial character in your child, this book will do just that. It will help you discover how, through daily family life, your child can learn the essential skills and attitudes to help them succeed in the future economy and, best of all, have lots of creative fun in the process!"

Mark Hibbitts, author of the *Alfie Potts the Schoolboy Entrepreneur* series of children's books

"I'm so excited to see *Enterprising Child* on the bookshelves; parents and children are going to love it. Lorraine was instrumental in the planning and running of our playgroup's activities, including arts, crafts, and singing. She knew how to engage the children in meaningful themed activities which were cost effective but also lots of fun – for adults as well as the children!"

Nicola Keay-John, mum to Darcey (5) and registered childminder

"Working with Lorraine over the past couple of months has been a massive help to my recent start-up confidence, as she listened very closely to the issues I was facing and offered expert advice in how I might tackle them, drawing from her own depth of knowledge and experience. As my children start to help me with the business, they are benefitting from what I've learnt by working with Lorraine and I know that, as a family, we're going to reap the rewards from the activities in this book."

Richard Baldock, owner of Desktag and dad to Harry (13) and Jack (16)

This book is dedicated to enterprising children around the world and to the parents and guardians of those children, in the hope that you will always retain a child-like sense of wonder in your life; also to my very own enterprising child, Dylan.

Acknowledgements

Through the course of writing this book, I have met many amazing people who have been so generous with their time, and prepared to share their stories of childhood, youthful ambitions, and parenting. Whether successful entrepreneurs, educators, aspiring entrepreneurs or parents going about their everyday lives in what they believe is an ordinary way, they are all doing something extraordinary.

I would like to make particular mention of Mary Cummings who, as well as lending an ear to my initial questions and ideas, came on board as a contributor to the book. Her work on the introductory chapter on the role of parents in developing children's entrepreneurial potential, the 9-11 and 11-14 activities and her help with the interviews has been invaluable.

In addition to thanking Tim Campbell MBE for his wonderful support and encouragement, I would like to acknowledge and say thank you to the following:

Aardman Animations; David Adjaye; Timothy Armoo; Louis Barnett; Julie Bishop; Claire Bolton; Adam Bradford; Alan Brooks, Head of External Affairs at The Aldridge Foundation; Zoe Brown; Kris Clarke; John and Sharon Cousins; Luke Cousins; Emily Cummins; Jasmine and Ben Cutting; Michael Davis, Chief Executive of the UK Commission for Employment and Skills; Priya Desai; Jamie Dunn; Danielle Ellis, primary school teacher; James Fothergill, Head of Education and Skills at CBI; James Headspeath; Kirsty Henshaw; Nicola Horlick; Paul Lindley; Annie Manning; Charlie Mayfield, Chairman of John Lewis Partnership; Claire Meredith; Georgina Moseley (for Harry); Jennifer Okpapi; Martin Rowland; Cheryl Ryder;

Ralph Scott at Demos; Soila Sindiyo; Laura Tenison MBE; Andrew Thrower, primary school deputy head; Enterprise Rockers for rocking the microbiz world while I've been writing; and, of course, to my husband Chris, for his endless patience and ability to be creative and enterprising whilst "Mum's working".

A final, big thanks to my publisher, Bookshaker, and in particular Lucy McCarraher, for such skill and patience in guiding me through each stage to reach this final production. Thank you for believing in *Enterprising Child*.

Contents

Foreword

There is a lot of pressure on parents nowadays to raise perfect children. Be they tiger mothers or helicopter fathers, the pursuit of the best way to empower our children to be the best can seem relentless and sometimes intimidating. As a parent I understand this, as I spent a lot of time wondering if what I was doing for my children was the best for them. From the right food to the right schools, I was always questioning if what I was doing was going to make them better. The problem with all this focusing on models of parenting is that there is no way to really tell if what we are doing is actually helping our children, as opposed to making us feel better, as the focus is on us as parents, not on our children as individuals. Once I moved my focus from trying to make them "better", to allowing their true selves to develop naturally – with guidance, of course – and realised that good enough parenting is about creating an environment where the person they are meant to be is allowed to grow, I actually found that parenting became much less of a worry and much more of a shared experience.

Through my experience in featuring in this book, and agreeing to write the Foreword, I was forced to reflect back on my own upbringing and the way my mum taught me and my siblings. I initially thought that much of what we learned was from the books she made us read and the focus she had on 'Education, Education, Education'. High level attainment in formal qualifications was very important to her and didn't we know it! But looking back now on my own path of dots that have joined up to lead me to where I am today, I can see that actually I took as much from watching her face and deal with the challenges life threw at her as a single parent as I did from her stern words about the grades I was going to get and the man I should aim to become. Don't get me wrong, I did very well in formal education, but the way Mum instilled in us pride, confidence and resilience through stories of family life back in Jamaica, as well as the importance of responsibility and diligence through chores and rewards, made her a better teacher than some of the lecturers I've had over the years, in terms of what has stayed with me and been most useful in the real world. Her ability to make us see the value of money by involving us in deciding what we needed on the weekly shop and the way she involved us in the upkeep of the family home made us not only very aware of our environment but, most importantly, our ability to influence it. I see now that her teaching through interaction was her own take on Newton's third law!

Now, as a father myself, what I actually want is for my children to be armed with skills and the right attitude to deal with the fast paced, ever changing world they are growing up in. I want them to be happy and independent (and for them not to forget me when I'm old would be nice too!). In order for that to happen, I think they have to be entrepreneurial. That doesn't necessarily mean business orientated, or preoccupied with material wealth, but entrepreneurial in the sense of being adaptable, inquisitive and open to taking calculated risks. For that's what I learned from my mum; that's what has served me well in the enterprises I have created and that's the gift I want to pass on to all of my children through our bloodline.

Mark Twain said that life does not consist mainly, or evenly largely, of facts and happenings. It consists mainly of the storm of thoughts that is forever blowing through one's head. *Enterprising Child* and the journey Lorraine wants to take us on as parents, guardians and/or teachers of the next generation will help make those thoughts imaginative and educational without being hard work. She also gives us additional tools, and in some cases acts as an aide memoir to things we know instinctively from our own childhood that work. But the main thing that reading this book will take away is the worry that our interaction with our children, whether we are rich or poor young or old, will be enough or more precisely *good* enough. I don't want perfect children. I just want children I can worry less about. Well, that is until my daughter starts dating and then I hope Lorraine writes a book on that topic too!

I hope you use this book to be even greater role models to your children and inspire them to be role models who are great.

Tim Campbell MBE

Introduction

WHY ENTERPRISING CHILD?

The inspiration for this book came about several years ago when I noticed that enterprise education in mainstream primary and secondary schools was gaining interest and momentum. I was, and still am, very much in favour of this, but it started me thinking about the role of parents in continuing that learning outside school, how parents might be supported to do that and how learning can take place through everyday situations or family activities in a fun way.

Roll forward several years and with the increased teaching of enterprise skills in school, it still seems important to address questions about the role of parents. As a business owner now, with a young son of my own, I decided it was the right time to explore further and find some answers. I searched for good quality and comprehensive resources for parents interested in developing their child's entrepreneurial potential in the broadest sense, i.e. not just about teaching them business skills, but couldn't find any. Enterprising Child – the book and website – was born.

WHO IS THIS BOOK FOR?

The book has been written primarily for parents (and of course anyone *in loco parentis* such as grandparents, child carers, educators, and so on) who are interested in developing children's entrepreneurial potential. It can also act as a very useful resource for individuals thinking about starting up a business or wondering whether they have 'what it takes' to do that as, although the activities are categorised according to the age of the child, the surrounding information about skills and attitudes required in business or the workplace will act as a useful guide against which they can assess themselves.

- Over a hundred ideas and plenty of inspiration to help you support the development of your child's entrepreneurial potential.
- Activities structured according to specific age groups.
- A clear understanding of what your child is learning at every stage.
- Non-prescriptive style which allows you to interpret and complete activities in a way that is appropriate for your child and situation.
- Inspirational interviews looking at the growing up years of successful entrepreneurs and business leaders and how they are developing their own children's entrepreneurial potential.
- Top tips for parents from entrepreneurs and business leaders.
- The connection between developing entrepreneurial character and employability.
- Access to a dedicated area of the Enterprising Child website.

HOW TO USE THIS BOOK

The book has been structured so you can easily dip in and out of sections – the activities, for example, are categorised according to age then into subject areas so you can focus on what is relevant to you. The book is intended to be used in conjunction with the Enterprising Child web site which will give you access to more resources, information and support.

LANGUAGE

For ease of reading and presentation, the word 'child' has been used throughout the book, but should be substituted with 'children' where that reflects your particular situation. Similarly the word 'parent' is used extensively but should be interpreted to mean anyone *in loco parentis.*

The word 'entrepreneur' is used generically to refer to someone actively involved in some stage of the process of creating or running their own business or social enterprise. 'Entrepreneurial', (used interchangeably with 'enterprising') as used here, however, describes the sort of person who *might* set up a business, but may also be entrepreneurial in the workplace as an employee. The interest here is the development of the sort of characteristics that can lead to not just success in business, but as an employee and in other areas of life.

ACTIVITIES

The activities and opportunities for learning presented in this book all follow the same structure: an introduction to the subject followed by suggested activities and ideas and finishing with a summary of what your child is learning by doing those activities.

INTERVIEWS

The interviews published throughout and at the end of the book provide an amazing insight into the growing up years of successful entrepreneurs or business leaders you may well have heard of. Rather than focus on how they built their businesses, I wanted to understand about their childhood, how their parents' or guardians' work ethics and values influenced decisions they went on to make about work and business and, where applicable, how they are developing their own children's entrepreneurial potential.

This book has not been written by parenting experts, so if you're wanting to learn about particular parenting skills or how to deal with the inevitable challenges associated with bringing up a child between the ages of 4 and 14 there are plenty of books out there — some of which are on my own bookshelf.

This book will also not provide you with a blueprint for guaranteed material success for your child. It goes beyond the populist notions of an entrepreneur to explore the wider concepts of what it means to be *entrepreneurial*, to enable you to support your child to help them think and act in a way that will help them make the best of the opportunities and challenges life presents whether as an employee or a business owner.

It is hoped that this book will help you add to your child's enjoyment of their childhood, and help them to develop their full potential, though it is not guaranteed to make them rich and famous. If it does I'll be back for a quote!

I know that parenting is one of the biggest challenges we will ever face in our lives. There is an enormous responsibility placed upon us in bringing up a child: helping them discover their passion and talents, develop the inner resources to face life's difficulties and make the most of its opportunities. All learning starts with play, and the capacity to be playful is a great way to facilitate learning, in ourselves as well as in our children. None of us wants to see our children grow up too soon and as adults we need to retain our capacity to play to help us learn too.

I hope that this book helps both you and your child to learn whilst having fun.

Lorraine Allman

What are the characteristics of an entrepreneur and why should they matter for your child?

If you've googled the word *entrepreneur* recently, you will know that there are hundreds of millions[2] of results returned world-wide and over eight million for the UK – stories of famous entrepreneurs, resources to support new start-up businesses, and entrepreneurial learning opportunities. Entrepreneurs and entrepreneurship can be defined in many ways.

Over recent years, populist notions portrayed through the media have developed the concept of what it means to be an entrepreneur. They often paint a glossy picture of an entrepreneur as wealthy (demonstrated through material objects such as numerous cars, holidays, yachts), having the Midas touch (everything they are involved with appears to succeed), with just the occasional nod to having put in the hours.

Not every child will want to run their own business when they're older, or indeed be the next Lord Sugar, Deborah Meaden, or Peter Jones, and as this book is about you as a parent supporting your child to think and act in a way that will help them make the best of the opportunities and challenges life presents, rather than providing a blueprint for guaranteed material success, we need to go beyond the populist notions and explore the wider concepts of what it means to be entrepreneurial.

[2] 137 million, June 2012

The *Oxford Dictionary*[3] defines an entrepreneur as *a person who sets up a business or businesses, taking on financial risks in the hope of profit.* We think this definition is too one-dimensional, and that it is important to recognise there can be different kinds of entrepreneur. A *Social Entrepreneur,* for example, is a founder and developer of a social enterprise whose primary goal is the pursuit of some social good through business trading and development, and very different from a *Commercial Entrepreneur* whose main goal in life appears to be to develop a profitable business, sell it, and move on to the next one, all the while amassing a personal fortune. These are both distinct from the *Lifestyle Entrepreneur* who turns a personal passion or interest into a business with the main aim of developing a lifestyle that enables them to pursue their interest and support themselves and their family in the process. These small *lifestyle* businesses (also known as micro-enterprises) make up the vast majority of businesses in the UK and research[4] has shown that very few actually recognise the term entrepreneur as being associated with what they do – i.e. building and running a sustainable small business.

Increasingly, the term *Intrapreneur* is used to recognise individuals who, whilst remaining as an employee in a company, use their entrepreneurial skills for that company's advantage without risking their own time and money.

Whatever people choose to call themselves or however they are referred to, it is the characteristics they share, rather than what differentiates them, which is the subject of this chapter. Here are five characteristics that we believe are key to defining the entrepreneurial individual. Each characteristic is a necessary foundation for the learning and development of relevant skills and, whilst the teaching of skills and knowledge can be pursued in many

[3] http://oxforddictionaries.com/definition/entrepreneur?q=entrepreneur
[4] http://www.sage.co.uk/news/who-are-you-calling-entrepreneur.html

settings, we recognise (and clearly you do too if you are reading this book), that we as parents are uniquely well placed to help develop our child's personality characteristics and habits of mind.

The key characteristics are referred to throughout this book to anchor the content and to keep a focus on the essential nature of the entrepreneurial mindset. In the age-appropriate activities in particular we will show how each characteristic and the associated skills, attitudes, and knowledge can be supported, encouraged, and nurtured in our children, but for now, let's look at each of the key characteristics in turn.

1. **Perceptions of possibilities**

   An entrepreneur perceives possibilities then takes the initiative in exploring and exploiting these in search of the realisation of *Value* (see characteristic number 5). In this sense the entrepreneur resembles an artist or visionary in seeing beyond the everyday, viewing things in a way that brings to light the possibilities and unrealised potential in situations.

   Skills and attitudes: Visionary, Intuitive, Critical Thinking, Autonomy, Sales mindset, Flexible, Innovative, Creative, Commercial awareness, Open-minded.

2. **Ambition**

   An entrepreneur will seek to change the status quo, to make a difference, whether through a new innovation or changing the way existing systems or products work; s/he wants to do things better and achieve more.

   Skills and attitudes: Self-motivating, Resilience, Perseverance, Competitive, Sales mindset, Self-belief.

3. **Risk and Resolve**

There are no risk averse entrepreneurs, just as there are no risk averse mountaineers – each has their own mountain to climb and must face risk in accepting the challenge. An entrepreneur will embrace risk and manage it in a way which demonstrates resolve in the same way that a climber will embrace risk, yet manage the risk of their next climb through checking their equipment and assessing their ability and mindset against the difficulty and degree of risk presented by that particular climb. Embracing risk doesn't mean they are not monitoring and/or calculating the exposure to risk and attempting to minimise it where possible.

Without the ability to take risks there is no enterprise and no summit. Without the ability to monitor and manage risk there are only failures, accidents, and fatalities.

Skills and attitudes: Self-motivated, Focused, Researcher, Risk taker, Decision maker, Resilience, Ability to work independently, Leadership, Self-reliant, Management of time and self, Adaptable, Flexible, Resilient, Energy, Autonomy, Self-belief.

4. **Teamwork**

Inspiring others and working in and leading teams is central to any entrepreneurial project. No matter how perceptive, ambitious, and resolute the individual, they are unlikely to succeed if they cannot move others to share their vision and co-operate in its realisation, quite often when the odds appear against them or there is little immediate obvious reward.

Skills and attitudes: Leader, Sales mindset, Team worker, Communicator, Listener, Adaptable, Flexible, Networking, Building relationships, Interpersonal, Preparedness to ask for help.

5. Value

An entrepreneur is a creator of value – someone who focuses on the end game, monitoring results whether for profit, social impact, or other measures of 'success'. In our economy value is frequently equated with profit, and the *bottom line* is a purely monetary concept, but as we saw in our description of different types of entrepreneurship, the creation of value is a wider and more fundamental notion than simply making money and may include the value inherent in, for example, the design and utility of goods and services, social and community benefits or the achievement of *the good life*, as defined by their individual aspirations – ethical, existential, spiritual, or material.

Skills and attitudes: Focused, Commercial awareness, Financial literacy, Preparedness to ask for help (puts value before pride).

SO WHY ARE ENTREPRENEURIAL CHARACTERISTICS IMPORTANT?
As we've already said, we're not suggesting that every child should start their own business or become an entrepreneur. We do believe, however, that encouraging, supporting, and nurturing your child to think and behave in an *entrepreneurial way* will have a significant impact on the way in which they view themselves, the world they live in and the opportunities and challenges they will inevitably face in the years ahead.

Regardless of whether the economic climate is a positive one or chaotic or deteriorating, we believe a young person brought up in a home where entrepreneurial characteristics are recognised, supported, and encouraged, along with the opportunity to learn key skills, will have a great advantage when seeking employment, business opportunities, or even business investment.

Evidence in the *'Enterprising employees of the future'* chapter shows that employers do not feel the education system adequately supports the development of entrepreneurial skills in young people. This research, combined with an analysis of the type of *employability* skills employers are looking for, indicates that entrepreneurial skills and attitudes are not just essential for potential new business owners, but also play an important part in young people succeeding in the world of employment. In an era of unprecedented high youth unemployment, those with entrepreneurial skills and attitudes will stand out as employers look for skills such as commercial awareness, a solution focused approach to problems, strong team working, and communication and interpersonal skills.

We are optimistic that over the coming years, initiatives and campaigns to support enterprise education in mainstream primary and secondary schools will start to address the apparent inadequacies; however, as parents, we have a crucial role in supporting and encouraging our children to make the best of themselves and their opportunities. We know that in the formation of personality and attitudes, which form the foundation for acquiring appropriate practical skills and knowledge, the parent's role, from the early years before formal education has even commenced, is absolutely crucial.

So, if you think that the five key characteristics of successful entrepreneurs identified here are appealing ones, and you want to give your child the opportunity to develop as a wise, creative and courageous shaper of their own destiny, we hope you will find

Enterprising Child an exciting and stimulating way to recognise and release your own inner entrepreneur and to nurture your child in a way that will allow them to be most authentically themselves, to be creators of value, not just passive consumers of the fruit of other people's efforts.

Your child's future is one of unrealised possibility; you will not always be able to protect or guide them, but you can do your best to give them the emotional bedrock and the experiences, attitudes and values now that will give them the best possible chance to make the best possible future for themselves and for others.

The role of parents in developing children's entrepreneurial potential

'Parents are the principal architects of a fairer society...'

Demos, 'Building Character' by Jen Lexmond and Richard Reeves, November 2009

This quote is taken from a report by Demos[5], an independent think-tank carrying out high quality, socially responsible research, investigating the development of *'character capabilities contributing to life chances and the factors influencing their development'* in children's early years. The research, funded by the Equality and Human Rights Commission, demonstrates just how big an impact parents can have on their children's character development and capabilities and helping them to develop important skills for life.

What a tremendous responsibility this places upon parents; a responsibility that parents instinctively rise to. From the moment children are born, parents take on the role of loving and patient teachers throughout their young lives. Parents recognise their role as nourishing their children's intellectual and emotional needs as well as those for food and sustenance.

So how can parents support their children with the all-important skills for working life? Are parents equipped to help their children develop those key characteristics and skills? Research carried out

---

[5] *'Building Character' by Jen Lexmond and Richard Reeves, November 2009. www.Demos.co.uk*

by the Aldridge Foundation in 2011[6] suggests that many feel they are not, with 88% of parents fearing for the job prospects for their children, and only 28% believing they were confident to help their children develop the essential skills to succeed in the job market.

Honor Wilson-Fletcher MBE, Chief Executive of the Aldridge Foundation said[7]:

> *Many parents hear words like entrepreneurial and risk and don't know how to help children develop these qualities. Unfortunately programs such as The Young Apprentice or Dragons' Den may give the impression that successful entrepreneurs are ruthless wheeler-dealers, simply in it for personal enrichment, and with little desire to work as a team, when the reality is quite different.*

Introducing at least the concept of employment and business in its many guises to younger children in preparing them for a future job market is as important as the introduction of ICT is in preparing them for a world led by information and technology. Speaking with business leaders and looking at outcomes of research by employer representative bodies such as the Confederation of British Industry and youth organisations such as Young Enterprise, it is clear that a considerable gap remains between the skills and attitudes of potential new young recruits and what employers are looking for[8]. Key areas, such as an ability to work in a team, to self-manage, problem solve, be an effective communicator and have commercial awareness are all considered essential and yet many companies are finding young people are leaving school without them.

As authors, parents, and business women ourselves, we believe

---

[6] *'Tips to develop effective skills for work' – Aldridge Foundation, November 2011*

[7] http://www.aldridgefoundation.com/news/aldridge-foundation-s-tips-to-develop-effective-skills-for-work

[8] Please read 'Enterprising employees of the future' chapter after the activities in this book for more information.

there is much that parents can do to prepare children to develop any of the key entrepreneurial characteristics they need to succeed in their working lives.

Through interviews with parents for this book we have found some wonderful examples of how parents are doing just that. For example, *Annie Manning* regularly involves her daughter Katie with her fundraising efforts and it was through volunteering for a local pet store that Katie secured a valuable work experience placement.

Laura Tenison MBE, who, as a child, developed an interest in sewing, was encouraged by her parents to pursue this and they gave her a sewing machine and the fabrics she needed for her hobby. This clearly played a part in encouraging Laura to follow her passion further and she later went on to form baby wear company *JoJo Maman Bébé*, which at the time of writing has a gross turnover of £31million.

Louis Barnett became one of the youngest people to set up a business, *Chokolit*, at the age of just 12 and says of his parent's influence

> *When finally I realised that I wanted to become a chocolatier and told my parents they both said they would support me in whatever career I chose as long as it was what made me happy. They both then set about buying small amounts of equipment so I would have the tools to begin working with chocolate. My father helped me research chocolate suppliers and this led to him booking a three-day training course... They both gave up their time to join in and learn too. They have supported my ideas and have provided a constant source of encouragement.*

John Cousins, a vet, encouraged his son Luke to help out when he brought home a client's sick budgerigar. Luke enjoyed the experience so much that he went on to regularly help out, in exchange for a little pocket money. It spurred in Luke a desire to take on bigger risks, to the extent that he began trading on eBay and at the age of only 14 created *VioVet*, an online pet medication and food store.

Parents do a vital job in supporting children with their learning: in numeracy not just by teaching their child how to count, but helping them to solve problems and think logically; in literacy by helping children to develop good communication skills – listening and talking has a direct bearing on a child's ability to read and write; and encouraging learning about themselves and the world around them through play, developing cognitive concepts *(what does this do/what will happen next?)*, and important social skills *(how to co-operate, negotiate, take turns)*. In all of this, parents are already having a direct impact on their children's educational, emotional and social development – not to mention their confidence.

But then there is that precious commodity, *time.* Are any of us able to fit anything else into our already hectic, time-strapped, over-scheduled lives? Through our own experiences and that of our interviewees, we have found the answer to be a resounding *yes.* Throughout the book you will see how easy it is to support, encourage, and nurture the five key entrepreneurial characteristics in your child through everyday activities and scenarios you're familiar with and have lots of fun in the process.

Introducing the activities

The activities have been categorised according to age, taking into account developmental milestones, and suggest how through everyday situations and activities you can support your child to develop their entrepreneurial potential.

Each activity refers back to at least one of the five entrepreneurial characteristics outlined previously, so you will see which particular skills, attitudes, and enterprising behaviour your child is learning. Further resources to support activities with your child are available at www.enterprisingchild.com.

All the parents interviewed have been generous in talking about the activities they carry out with their children and have provided real inspiration and encouragement to us; we are very grateful to them for that.

There are just a few things we should mention before you dive in:

PACE SETTING AND ROUTE
Whilst the activities have been categorised according to age, it's important that your child sets the pace at which they learn and that their innate curiosity to find out more, even if that means going 'off route', takes precedence over rigid conceptions of age appropriateness.

Whatever their stage of development, or individual abilities, and accepting that all children are different, it is important that your child's desire to know more is supported, so put aside anxieties about where you think they *should* be on the developmental path, as this will inevitably create stress for you and your child and inhibit their learning.

Every child is unique and therefore finding the style of language and interaction to suit your own situation and child is really important. The activities are not prescriptive in saying there is any one way to do things – you know your child better than anyone, and each family will have its own micro-culture, communication styles and ways of encouraging learning.

WHEN THINGS DON'T GO ACCORDING TO PLAN
The activities presented here are simply suggestions of how you might want to carry out activities or discuss situations with your child. Particular activities may not work out as planned (especially the practical craft or experimental ones) so the crucial issue is how that is dealt with. For example, rather than seeing the activity as having failed, you could work with your child to try to understand why it didn't turn out as expected and encourage them to try again. Asking questions such as *'Why do you think that happened?'* or *'What could be done differently?'* will help them learn from mistakes and not be afraid to carry on experimenting.

Alternatively, or in addition, focus on the positive aspects of what has been achieved, viewing the end result as a new invention. This approach to what might be viewed as a failed task encourages your child to learn through an evaluative process. That's not to say that failure in itself is a negative thing; many now successful entrepreneurs have 'failed' businesses behind them and believe the learning from that was more valuable than from anything else.

FOLLOW MY LEADER

Whenever possible, taking into account risk (see below), encourage your child to take the lead in an activity or at the very least give them responsibility for particular tasks.

With their natural curiosity and energy levels, children can become very engaged in specific areas of interest (this is particularly true of children on the autistic spectrum), so if you see that happening encourage them to develop their interest and help them set small, achievable goals to encourage learning and progression, whether with computers, caring for animals, drawing, collecting, or whatever takes their fancy.

RISK TAKING

Any activities carried out with children carry a degree of risk, even the simplest things can catch us out, but a life without risk would be a boring one indeed. Concerns are now being expressed that the current generation of children is not developing essential skills like calculating risks and resilience because of a desire to minimise risk, resulting in 'cotton wool kids'[9]. We are not suggesting that your young child should be out climbing trees without supervision, but involving them in the planning and decision making process as part of the higher risk activities will help them to learn to appreciate and deal with risk, while not preventing the adventurous side of their nature being explored and developed.

SPECIAL NEEDS

Through interviewing parents and entrepreneurs, it became clear that in addition to contending with the usual demands of growing up, a number of them also had to deal with their children's or their own special needs. 'Special needs' covers a diverse range of areas,

---

[9] http://www.netmums.com/coffeehouse/general-coffeehouse-chat-514/news-current-affairs-topical-discussion-12/707694-cotton-wool-kids-1-5-do-not-play-out.html

so if your child has particular needs in any physical, emotional, intellectual, or social development aspect, how can you as a parent help them develop the enterprising characteristics to equip them for the world of business and employment?

As a parent of a child with special needs, you may already be working closely with your school or other appropriate professionals to identify your child's strengths and draw up an individual plan where they may need support. *Claire Bolton*, a Speech and Language Therapist based in London's Harley Street, had this to say about her experience with parents who approach her for support:

'Having a child is life-changing enough, but having a child with special needs suddenly throws parents into a new world of additional challenges and responsibilities. Most parents will not have had previous experience with special needs and may initially feel overwhelmed by a diagnosis – although many parents are also relieved to finally have a label that describes their children's difficulties.

'It is vital to always remember that a label is merely that – just a label. A diagnosis is not a prognosis and all children, regardless of ability, constantly need to have others believe in their potential to progress, focusing on strengths rather than limitations.

The variation in types of disabilities is enormous. A diagnosis is simply a way to categorise difficulties, but within these categories all children possess unique and delightful characteristics. Every child, regardless of their 'label', has incredible potential to reach the best of their ability.'

The activities are designed to be flexible according to your own situation and the needs of your child. There are some great examples of parents who use highly practical techniques to encourage their child's entrepreneurial potential where that child has particular special needs. What works for one child of course may not work for another, but the encouraging thing is that all the parents who have children with special needs agreed that focusing on and building upon their individual strengths brought tangible results in helping them reach their potential.

BE A MODEL

One key thing that emerged from our many different interviews is that children learn as much if not more from your own behaviour as a parent than from school, books, computer games, or friends. As you will know from perhaps occasionally letting slip a word you might wish you hadn't, children learn quickly how to imitate both good and less positive behaviours and it is what they see us do, far more than what we tell them they should do, that they are most likely to internalise and base their behaviour upon.

We hope you and your child enjoy and find inspiration from the activities which follow. Above all we encourage you to have lots of fun.

Activities for children aged 4-6 years

I will fix you – doing things better

Creative beyond the craft

Conflict – we can work it out

Enterprising play

Planning it out

Selling it like it is

The art of storytelling

Money doesn't grow on trees – or does it?

Manufacturing

Giving it back

I will fix you – doing things better

Passion is about exploring with your child what really gets to them in terms of interest. Tenacity, well that's about going the extra mile, to be persistent and think about how things can be better next time around. Ella and I say 'What do quitters do? They quit'. It's important to encourage them to go the extra mile to do the extra thing which will achieve results.

Paul Lindley, founder of Ella's Kitchen and dad to Ella (12) and Paddy (9)

Entrepreneurs aren't always creators of innovative new products. They often simply seek to improve what is already in the market by changing the way existing systems, services, or products work. Through this desire to improve and make a difference they will also embrace risk and manage it in a way which demonstrates resolve, so it is important to encourage your child to start thinking about opportunities for change for the better, and not be concerned about 'getting it wrong'. Your support in discussing ideas, however wacky, with your child; helping them discover what works and what doesn't, will show them that their opinions are valued even if the ideas don't work out or aren't suitable.

It's easy as a parent to be the fixer when even minor incidents with young children occur. Take, for example, knocking over a drink or tripping over an object. Fixing the problem (mop up/remove the offending object) and moving on is often the quickest solution, but even these situations can provide you with an opportunity to encourage your child to develop an attitude of finding or creating solutions for themselves. For example, which type of material works best for mopping up spillages, where might the object be better placed? You may need to prompt your child, but it's highly likely their own imagination will soon get to work and they'll be coming up with lots of ideas and suggestions to reduce the number of incidents occurring.

ACTIVITIES

Queues

Queuing is a fact of life – at least in Britain! – but the next time you're stuck in a queue with your child and tempted to check your watch, or sigh under your breath, have a chat with them about what they think could be done to make the queue move more quickly. Here's an example of how one mum turned an unexpectedly long wait for food into an opportunity to discuss business processes and solutions to the situation:

> *On the way home from a swimming lesson the other day with my five year old son I stopped off at the drive-through as we do every Thursday. The queue of cars was unusually long and my son his usual hungry self. To pass the time, I asked why he thought it was so busy today and whether he could think of anything the company could do to make the queue move faster. He gave some thoughtful responses wondering whether perhaps one of the 'food machines' had broken down and commenting that maybe there weren't enough staff.*

This kind of questioning and discussion not only helped to pass the time waiting in the queue, but also took the child's mind off his hunger and encouraged him to come up with ideas, thinking about some of the processes involved in his food arriving, e.g. machines, and people. When he had talked about what might have happened to create the queues, he was then encouraged to think about possible solutions to the problem.

...he said he thought that there should be at least one person in the company who knew how to fix the machine if it had broken and that there should be a back-up one anyway. When I asked him about staff he replied, 'There should be more'. However, when I explained maybe the company couldn't afford any more his response was 'Well then they need to make the ones here smile more'. I'm guessing he was thinking that a smile goes a long way when people have been waiting a while – I couldn't argue with that!

The soggy sandwich
School lunchboxes can be a challenge for many parents, particularly if you have a fussy eater, but what happens when your child regularly arrives home saying '*I couldn't eat my sandwich it was all soggy*'? There are a number of ways to approach this. For example, you could simply explore with your child alternative lunches such as pasta and decide how that should be stored to stay fresh; or you could talk about *why* the sandwiches go soggy and what could be done to keep them crisper.

Encourage them to think about what other foods change when left for a few hours out of the fridge – e.g. pizza becomes chewy – then google '*how to stop sandwiches going soggy*'[10] to see what solutions people have already thought of. This is great experience for learning that entrepreneurial thinking isn't always about coming up with a new idea but building on what is already out there in the market.

Chief experimenter
It's surprising how many experiments your child can safely carry out either by themselves or with a little supervision using basic items in kitchen cupboards such as flour, eggs, vinegar, food colouring,

[10]Around 702,000 results June 2012

salt, and water. Yes, it's likely to be messy, but clearing up is part of the learning process too. Some experiments they might like include making salt dough, floating an egg, or creating volcano lava. All these and more are available on the Enterprising Child website[11].

The key with this kind of activity is experimentation. If something doesn't work and they end up with a stodgy mess (easily done if the measurements are wrong for salt dough), ask your child what could be done differently (e.g. more salt) and encourage them to try again.

Your work
Whether you work for someone else or run your own business, try to include your child in conversations about your work, especially if there are small problems that need solving – e.g. you keep running out of stamps or the clocking-in system regularly breaks down. Discussions over the dinner table can work well where everyone contributes ideas and your child can learn how we all approach problem solving differently. A young child's more simplistic view of a problem can be incredibly enlightening for adults and you may well end up with a surprisingly workable solution.

[11]www.enterprisingchild.com

WHAT YOUR CHILD IS LEARNING

Approaching everyday situations such as queuing and soggy sandwiches, and experimenting with kitchen basics provides opportunities for your child to start learning about possibilities and potential. Through their willingness to experiment and take risks, trying out new ideas as many times as necessary to achieve the desired result, their ambition to do things better and achieve more value can be realised.

Encouraging your child to focus less on the problem and more on finding a solution develops their creative thinking abilities as well as problem-solving skills. Being able to effectively communicate those ideas is important in order for them to gain understanding so that others can help (where appropriate) to make those solutions a reality. The experimentation activities are crucial in learning that there is no shame in making errors, and how, through trying again, they may even improve on the original idea.

Creative beyond the craft

The OED definition of 'creativity' is *'the use of imagination or original ideas to create something; inventiveness'* and there is no shortage of activities for young children to get involved in which use their imagination, creating anything from painted pictures to planting seeds and watching their gardens grow. If, however, we think more widely than just the arts and crafts and consider ways to encourage creative *thinking* as opposed to creative *doing* then there are endless possibilities for helping children understand social relationships and to go beyond the everyday.

ACTIVITIES

Word association

A word association game can be fun for all the family, whether at the meal table or when friends come calling. Let your youngest child start with a word and the person next to them says a word they associate with the one your child has given. Move around the group with each person saying a word they associate with the previous one and so on, until it is your child's turn again. Keep going round for as long as you wish. What this game shows is the inter-connectedness of concepts, and demonstrates in an implicit way the interaction between linguistic conventions and personal interpretation; the way in which we each can create novelty and uniqueness from something as apparently defined and conventional as linguistic meaning.

Putting my own spin on it

It's all too easy to have expectations as to how our children will behave in accordance with what is considered the norm, based in part on our own experiences and desires. A case in point below:

Every year we have a fabric advent calendar with 24 pockets containing different animals, characters, and items from the nativity story. Starting on 1ˢᵗ December, my son carefully takes one item out of its pocket and places it on the main canvas, over the course of the next 24 days creating his own 'nativity scene'. Last year, aged five, something completely unexpected happened. The calendar came out as usual but instead of placing one item on the canvas each day, he took them all out to create a picture then one by one as each day passed put them back in their fabric pockets according to the story he wished to tell.

I have to admit it took all my strength not to interfere; I was really struggling with the fact that he chose to 'tell' the story in a different way to what I expected, plus of course the end result was not a picture on the canvas but a story told according to where the items had been placed in their pockets.

Eventually I realised that my struggle said more about my inability to accept something other than the 'norm' than it did about my son's decision to do something different, and it has taught me a big lesson in learning to let go of my preconceptions and to trust my child to experiment and discover his own creative approach to storytelling.

Lorraine, mum to Dylan (5½)

Storytelling

Talking of storytelling, this is a great way to encourage creative thinking in your child. *The art of storytelling* section has many ideas for activities which encourage them to get involved in creating their own or building on other's stories. A good resource to encourage the use of imagination in storytelling, particularly if your child is quite visual, is *Rory's Story Cubes*[12]. The cubes are a very portable

[12]http://www.amazon.co.uk/The-Creativity-Hub-Rorys-Story/dp/B003NFJMBM/ref=sr_1_1?s=kids&ie=UTF8&qid=1338740169&sr=1-1

resource and can be used if you're on a long journey or just want to make your own family entertainment. They are great for younger children who have less developed reading abilities.

Children who are confident in letter formation and handwriting could start their own storybook. Keep it simple, with a little notebook of their choice, and support them in jotting down notes to help develop the story such as character development (names, what the main characters look like and so on) and themes (what the story is about).

From curious to curiouser

Young children are naturally curious, so exploring events and possibilities with them can help their learning and ability to think creatively as well as give you an insight into how the world is viewed through their eyes.

Opportunities to experiment – see the *Fix you* section – will enable your child to explore the *what happens if..?* scenario using different kitchen ingredients, but they may just like experimenting through questions so be prepared to deal with lots of these. According to a survey[13], four out of five UK parents have been stumped by something their children have asked so, unless you're the lucky one out of five, continue to encourage your child's questioning as a natural extension of their curiosity and interest in life and work with them to discover the answer (even if that does mean googling it, not such a bad thing as it demonstrates the social nature of knowledge, that parents are not omniscient and that we should not expect ourselves to have all the answers).

Curiosity in young children ranges from the practical to the metaphysical. You can encourage your child to think through solutions to everyday situations, for example how to brighten up

[13]http://news.bbc.co.uk/1/hi/8200022.stm

the day when it's cold, wet, and wintry outside (responses might include turning the heating up, wearing summer clothes, eating ice cream, or drawing pictures of a rainbow). You can also encourage your child by taking seriously their questions about why things are as they are, where things come from, even why there are 'things' or anything at all.

The arty creative
There is a plethora of resources available in books or online for children of this age which focus on arts and crafts, far too many to be listed here and you may already have your favourites – in which case visit the Enterprising Child website and share them with us so they can be added to the resources available there.

Many children are also natural inventors and just love to build machines, rockets and all sorts of weird and wonderful stuff from the many construction kits and toys available for all ages, but here are eight of our top arts and crafts resources – a combination of books and websites – which have been chosen for their age appropriateness, breadth of activities and requiring (in the main) simple, everyday materials found around the home or which can be bought for minimal cost.

Green crafts for children by Emma Hardy, published by CICO Books, 2011

365 things to make and do (Usborne activities) published by Usborne Publishing Limited, 2007

Creative Crafts for Kids: Over 100 Fun Projects for Two to Ten Year Olds by Gill Dickinson, published by Hamlyn, June 2009

Garden Crafts for Children by Dawn Isaac, published by CICO Books 2012

Playtime activities by Ray Gibson, published by Usborne Publishing Limited, 1998

Little Hands Art Book: Exploring Arts and Crafts with 2- to 6-year Olds (Little Hands!) (Williamson Little Hands Book) published by Ideals Publishing Corporation, U.S. 2008

Activity village[14]

Kaboose[15]

WHAT YOUR CHILD IS LEARNING

Encouraging your child's natural creativity provides a great opportunity for you to help them develop their perception of new possibilities. The essential characteristics being developed are both the innate thoughtfulness and imaginative engagements with the world and the possibilities it presents, and also the willingness to experiment, indeed to fail and try again, that is an essential characteristic of the entrepreneurial spirit.

Teamwork is also relevant to creativity. Creativity is not always, probably not often, the province of the lone artist, engineer, or inventor, but is frequently a social pursuit that involves a willingness to share ideas and learn from others, and ultimately to inspire others with your vision.

---

[14]http://www.activityvillage.co.uk/
[15]http://crafts.kaboose.com/

Conflict – we can work it out

Whether at school or at home, at some point your child will experience conflict. It itself, conflict doesn't have to be negative, indeed in many ways the potential for conflict demonstrates our unique individuality. However, learning ways to deal with conflict effectively, with or without support, which respects differences will help your child to have the skills and confidence to handle disagreements as an adult.

Conflict happens for all sorts of reasons and is often related to individual preferences, e.g. your child wants to play a different game but their classmate/sibling doesn't. Conflict is present almost every day for young children, especially during playtimes, and they need help with the skills and confidence to be able to try resolving such situations, for themselves.

ACTIVITIES

Sibling/playtime conflict

This is probably one of the most common times for conflict at home either with siblings or visiting children. When things get too much it's easy for parents to find a quick resolution to the conflict without involving the children: 'You go and play in the lounge and Steven can play at the kitchen table.' The difficulty with this approach is that it doesn't involve the children in negotiating through the conflict so they are not learning key skills such as listening, negotiating, and respecting differences.

> *Conflict in the school playground is almost a daily occurrence, especially at this age. We believe it's important that children are involved in finding solutions to the problem so if, for example, one child has hurt another in the playground and they're both upset, we would encourage them to find a space (within sight) for*

'quiet time' where they sit together and talk it out. They come back to us when they have sorted the problem.

Danielle Ellis, primary school teacher

There's no reason why this collaborative approach to resolving conflict can't be taken at home too, where the children are encouraged to come up with solutions to the problem, to try and resolve the conflict, which may of course include an element of compromise. To begin with you may want to sit down with them and note down some of the ideas they come up with, which can then be discussed and compromise/consensus reached.

Competing for the same resources

In a family of more than one child, another common conflict scenario is when too many children want to play with the same thing. An alternative approach to simply removing the offending item is to ask the children to think about what else they might play with if that particular item wasn't there. Encourage them to consider whether they would enjoy the other possibilities as much or even more. Again, involving them directly in the conflict resolution process, asking them to think of ways in which they can ensure everyone has a chance to play with the item, will help them learn strategies for resolving the situation. If they're really stuck for ideas, especially in the younger age range, then help them with suggestions from simple things such as turn taking through to putting a rota together, but the more they come up with and put ideas into practice themselves, the more they will not just learn about, but become more confident in, handling situations of conflict.

Deal making

The desire for independence, even at this young age, can lead to occasional, sometimes frequent, battles of wills when it comes to trying to get things done. Reasoning doesn't really play a part at this age, but if there is some flexibility around what you want doing (remember it's best to pick your battles!) then a spot of deal making might just work for both parties.

Learning to negotiate and 'do a deal' is something that children start to learn about now and it can offer a way to work through actual or impending conflict at home. You can model the deal-making process to enable them to understand how it works, but it's up to you to set the boundaries as to when deals can and can't be made!

Asking for help

One of the most popular pieces of advice given to anyone starting a business or a new job is to ask for help. No one can be expected to know what they don't know and there is absolutely no shame in asking for assistance. This is an important lesson for young children to learn in dealing with conflict where it isn't possible to resolve a situation on their own and they need to know others are there to support them. 'Others' in that sense may not always mean adults, as this dad of a five year old explains:

> *Last December I took my son to a local soft play centre. He's a quiet child and would generally walk away from potential situations of conflict with other children, letting those who 'push in' just get on with it and walk away to a different part of the play area. This time, however, was different. He wanted to play in the section where the giant bouncing balls were but there was an older girl, probably eight or nine years old standing in his way and wouldn't let him through. He could have perhaps tried to*

negotiate with her, but given she was a good few years older he went off and found some of his friends of a similar age and asked them for help. By all accounts, it seems they chatted between them about what to do then all four approached the girl asking to go into the ball area. The girl moved aside.

WHAT YOUR CHILD IS LEARNING

Conflict in the workplace or in business is an inevitable part of working life and those adults who as a child learned the skills to deal with this, as opposed to avoid or simply not know how to deal with it, will be far better placed to handle difficult situations when they arise in work.

The preparedness to ask for help in resolving conflict is part of what characterises someone who is a creator of Value – they put potential value before personal pride. The ability to remain open minded to possible solutions and be flexible when it comes to compromise is an essential trait of the entrepreneur who can perceive possibilities and then secure the co-operation of others to create an environment for effective teamwork.

Enterprising play

The opportunities for your child to learn about different aspects of business and enterprise through their play activities; whether setting up a play shop or just kicking a ball around, are immense. What is important, however, is that as well as ensuring they are having lots of fun, you take the time to notice what appears to spark an interest in your child. Can you work out what it is about particular activities they enjoy? Is it, for example, the social interaction, the manufacturing element, the creative aspect, team working, helping others, the sales process, or a combination of these or other elements?

Noticing over time what your child enjoys can help you learn more about talents they may be developing; it gives you the opportunity to provide positive feedback and help them recognise and celebrate their own special talents. The key here is to ensure a variety of play activities and be guided by them as to what they want to focus on.

ACTIVITIES
Role play
Role play continues to be very popular at this age and is great for stimulating imagination and social interaction.

There are so many possibilities with role play at home, from gardening centres (use plant pots, seed packets) to furniture shops; from estate agents to clothes shops and cafes (cold drinks, cakes). Let their imagination have free play and make sure roles are rotated to experience the different sides of buying and selling.

If you have more than one child, get them all involved, and where, for example, they are setting up a café making drinks, introduce them to teamwork and learning how to organise tasks to get the job done (who is taking orders, making the order, washing up) as well as understanding different customer requirements.

Dylan dressed up in his best clothes and took great pride in showing me around our house... They both love to role play and each time they do they are developing an awareness about, and their own understanding of, different jobs and roles in society.

Claire Meredith, mum to Dylan (5) and Lloyd (2)

Chicken and egg

Do you, or does someone you know nearby, keep chickens? Find out whether your child could help to make an *Eggs for sale* sign or even help with selling them to other neighbours in return for a small fee per sale made (otherwise known as *commission sales*). If chickens and eggs aren't possible, try something else such as growing seedlings to sell or give away, where your child can help display them and make a suitable sign.

Dog walking

If you already own a dog then your child will know how important it is for it to be exercised every day. If they already accompany you on the dog walks, why not find out whether neighbours have dogs which need walking in return for a small fee, to be split with your child when they take part in the walk. Dog walking is a popular way of making a little money for older children, but there's no reason why, with your support, your younger child can't benefit from this too.

Car boot sales

Car boot sales are mentioned in *Selling it like it is* as a great example of getting your child involved in the different aspects of selling, but whether you hold a sale on your front driveway or take unwanted items to a car boot sale, getting your child involved from the start will give them a good introduction to the whole business process of buying and selling, from selection of goods to pricing, sales presentation, marketing, and customer service.

Award winning activities

The next time a local show takes place, find out whether there are categories for young children to enter. A local show could offer plenty of opportunities for children aged four and upwards to get involved in activities such as cooking, painting or even making an animal out of vegetables! This will give your child a boost by just seeing their products or designs on the table ready for judging. They may not win a prize, but that is true in business and enterprise as well – not every business succeeds or wins awards, but the most important thing is they have tried (you can always make your own little rosette to give them for entering and don't forget to take a photograph of their entry on the table) and can learn from the competition (other entries) what they could do differently next time, as one parent explains here

I realised when my son turned four that he was old enough to enter the local Agricultural Society County Show. We looked through the categories together to decide if there were any he wanted to enter. He loves to bake so I wasn't surprised he chose to make 'chocolate crispy cakes on a paper plate.' He also decided to enter a painting under the theme of 'Sunlight' and create a paper plate fish.

Making everything was good fun and he was so excited taking the entries over before the show opened, it made him feel very important! We visited the show on the final day to discover he had won second prize for the crispy cakes and painting, and highly commended for the paper plate fish. What surprised me most was how much time he spent looking at the entries which won first prize. When I asked him why he was doing that he said 'so I can see why they're better than mine and I can win first prize next time.

Helping neighbours

Getting your child involved in 'business' activities doesn't always have to mean they directly benefit financially. In the same way that an *in kind* approach to understanding the value of money can be taken (see *Money doesn't grow on trees – or does it?*), so learning that helping others can be equally rewarding is also important. *Giving it back* offers specific ideas for young children to learn social entrepreneurialism, but activities involving helping others may include going to visit an elderly neighbour or relative, or making a card for a friend who is unwell.

Your work

If you run your own business, find ways to get your child involved in it on a regular basis. At this age they are likely to be curious about what you do (and sometimes a bit annoyed if you have to answer the phone for business when you said you'd play with them!) so the more you can involve them the more opportunities there are for them to learn what it's all about.

Simple administrative tasks, such as putting stamps on envelopes, going to the post office with you, or putting paper in the printer, can get them involved with minimal responsibility.

If you have a job which takes you out and about to exhibitions or talks, show your child how you prepare for this. If you can, get them to help out with packing crates of your products or marketing leaflets. If you work in a shop, point out to your child all the different things you do to make the store look inviting to customers.

WHAT YOUR CHILD IS LEARNING

Entrepreneurs are usually very passionate individuals. It is clear from the way they speak that they are doing what they believe in, with a passion that sets them apart from others. We could say that the entrepreneur has retained their capacity for play – they share with children a sense of wonder, excitement, imagination, and total absorption in a project. It is hardly surprising that play is such a crucial factor in developing all the entrepreneurial characteristics identified, as it is the cornerstone of child development. If you want your child to learn useful lessons, make sure they are fun.

Planning it out

An ability to plan, to follow through and make decisions are essential entrepreneurial skills. Some people consider themselves an 'ideas person', preferring others to turn their ideas into reality, but an individual's ability to take an idea and work it through (with support from others where necessary) into something real, can make the difference between simply having plenty of good ideas with nothing to show or a real understanding of whether those ideas can be realised and how best to achieve them.

The following activities focus, not just on making plans, but ensuring that the follow-through takes place.

ACTIVITIES

Make a family planner

Involving your child in creating a weekly or monthly family planner can be lots of fun. The idea is to get everyone sitting around the table, agreeing who is doing what and when, so there will need to be some negotiating, especially if the plan is to create a rota of house chores. If you have a very young family, try to ensure the allocated tasks area easily achievable, ideally without support from you, e.g. tidying their room. If your child is not yet confident with letter forming and writing, encourage them to draw pictures to illustrate tasks.

An activity planner detailing who is doing what and when will require discussion focusing on responsibility and teamwork.

Whichever type of planner you create, take time to review as a family how the plan actually worked out and discuss whether anything could be done differently next time. This will help your child understand that sometimes even the best laid plans don't always work out first time, and that being flexible (which can be difficult for young children) is an essential element of carrying out plans.

Family trip

The next time you're going out on a trip together, get your child involved in the planning process. Once you've agreed where you're going and what you're doing, work with your child to decide on what's going in the packed lunch, what clothes to wear or take, or even get them involved in planning the route. Help your child with making a list which they could then put in order and allocate tasks to particular members of the family including themselves. The list can be as long or as short as your child is happy with, ranging from what needs to happen before you leave (e.g. feed the dog, close the windows) to responsibilities during the journey, on the activity, and even on return, for example who will be cleaning the muddy wellington boots?

Party party

Children of this age often love to go to a party, so why not encourage them to organise one at home for the immediate family. They can decide whether to hold it inside or outside, have a small budget to purchase balloons or party poppers, make up notices and invitations, plan the music and any games, and even have a few nibbles and soft drinks. It sounds a lot to organise, but let them take the lead and be around to offer support if needed. Planning a party at home provides a great opportunity for your child to develop their decision making skills as well as beginning to understand that events don't just happen on their own and how decisions are taken.

Meal planning

Encouraging your child to get involved in planning family meals will not only help them to understand a wide range of aspects related to meal planning such as food shopping, cooking, dietary requirements, likes and dislikes and so on, but also has the potential to get them more interested in a variety of food, which can be helpful if you have a fussy eater.

Understanding different members of the family's likes and dislikes will give them an insight into decisions that have to be made about buying ingredients, time needed to cook different meals, and perhaps reasons why everyone is encouraged to eat the same unless dietary necessities prohibit this.

Make-it!
If you have a child who loves to make things from disused and recycled materials, this is a great opportunity to teach them planning skills. Encourage them to plan the activity in advance using a simple design sheet[16] where they can draw or write what they will need e.g. egg boxes, paint, glue, pipe cleaners then draw what they think the model will look like. Through this process they are coming up with an idea, considering the resources needed to carry it out and identifying where help is required. If your child isn't keen on using the design sheet, there are lots of other ways for them to plan out the activity, such as use of simple spider diagrams or mind maps – these can be particularly useful if your child thinks visually.

Don't forget when they've completed their project ask them to tell you about it as opposed to asking *'What's that, then?'* which will allow them to talk about the process of making it and to evaluate how well the planning process worked.

There are a range of resources available to download from the Enterprising Child web site to help you with the activities featured here.

[16]Available to download from the Enterprising Child website

WHAT YOUR CHILD IS LEARNING

Entrepreneurial thinking isn't just about having good ideas, it's about perceiving how those ideas can be turned into reality, identifying the resources required, and securing the help of others when required. It needs an understanding of potential risks and precautions that can be taken, with the resolve to carry plans through from start to finish.

Achieving value through harnessing ambition requires focus, and it is in planning that entrepreneurs really learn the need for dealing with both strategy and operational detail and make key decisions to ensure success.

In these activities your child is beginning to learn about the nature and importance of planning, how to identify what resources might be needed to complete a task and organising co-operative effort within the family team.

Selling it like it is

Buying and selling is a core part of business life so it's never too early to help our children begin to understand the sales process. Many successful entrepreneurs either have excellent sales skills themselves or have recruited people as part of their team who excel at sales, so recognising and understanding the importance of sales is crucial to developing that entrepreneurial way of thinking and behaving.

ACTIVITIES
Shopping trips
Shopping trips provide plenty of opportunities to talk about consumer choice, pricing, customer service, and much more. The next time you're out shopping with your children, talk with them about particular shops and/or products you like and why. This kind of discussion will start to uncover more about why people shop the way they do, including issues such as consumer choice, customer service, pricing, knowledge of products, and environment.

I take time to talk [about] everyday experiences such as going food shopping… about why customer service may have been poor or why food took too long to arrive.

Zoe Brown, mum to Naomi (21), Xander (7), Evan (5), Hollie (2), and Abie (1)

Home shopping delivery
Do you have a regular supermarket delivery to your home? This can be an excellent opportunity for your child to learn about the online sales process (ordering and fulfilment), and give them a better

understanding of how you spend money and what items cost. The process can be followed through when the order arrives at home so they can see, with your help, whether anything has been substituted (if so whether that is accepted and why), and the total amount of money spent.

Playing shop
Follow up a home shopping delivery or shopping trip with a pretend shop game where you swap roles between shopper and shopkeeper. The role of shopkeeper is to set out the display of items – use items from your kitchen cupboards or around the house depending on the type of shop it is. Encourage your child to help you make decisions about what to buy, through describing items in terms of their benefits (e.g. this sofa is so comfy; it will look perfect next to your chair) rather than features.

Another new toy
Your child's play area may be full of toys, but when you're out and about they'll always spot something they like the look of and beg you to buy. Assuming you're happy in principle to buy the item, try some sales role play with them which builds on the activity above regarding benefits. For example, you could ask your child to give you reasons why you should buy what they want. They will gradually learn the art of persuasion and recognise that there has to be a benefit on both sides to win the argument, such as in this example:

> *My five year old used to say she wanted a new toy because she liked it, but quickly learned with a bit of support that there had to be more compelling reasons for me to buy her the toy than that. Now she says she'll sort through her toys and give one away if I buy her a new one, which then of course makes it hard to say no to!*

This can be a good way to introduce the difference between *benefits* and *features* in an informal way. *Features*, in sales language, refers to facts about the item being sold, and *benefits* to what the item gives to the consumer, so if your child says they want a toy because it has a flashing light, you could ask *why* this is appealing to them.

Car boot sales
Car boot sales are very popular in the UK. They offer a great way to get your child involved in many aspects of the buying and selling process, including areas such as deciding how much to charge for items through to display, dealing with customers, and handling cash. If they have decided they'd like to sell some of their own toys, you could provide a small table or allocate a section of yours for which they are responsible (under supervision).

Even if you're not running your own stall, car boot sales are great places to have a look around and see what other people are selling. Encourage your child to have a look around, see how much items are priced at, and to watch how buyers and sellers interact. A way to introduce the notion of making profit from a sale is to give them say £1 or £2 to buy something from the sale then have a go at selling it on (ideally at a profit) either back at your own stall or on an auction site such as eBay. Discuss with your child ways in which they could improve the value of the item for example by cleaning it up or fixing it if it's broken.

Farmers markets
Farmers markets are accessible, friendly places where you'll find local farmers ready and willing to have a chat to your child about how they've produced their stock – from vegetables and cheeses to meat, honey and more. Encourage your child to look at how each stall is laid out to encourage shoppers to buy, and look at which

stalls are easiest to walk into for a browse. Let your child complete the sales transaction themselves on a stall which has produce you know they like.

eBay/local sale

Somewhere between the ages of four and six your child is likely to be moving up a gear when it comes to the bike or scooter they're using. Suggest that they consider the different ways in which they could sell their current bike/scooter, for example you could help them complete the eBay process to sell it online. Think about the way in which the item is described to make it appealing (without misrepresenting of course) and look at other similar items on sale to determine the best start price if auctioning, or *buy it now* price. Alternatively, you might decide to sell the bike/scooter locally outside your house, so, again, do some research with your child on how much it should be sold for, and get them involved in making the sign as well as demonstrating the item to potential customers. It's all great experience and they're learning quickly about the many different aspects of the sales process as well as understanding how to interact with customers.

Your work

Where your work involves any aspect of the sales process, talk with your child about what that involves in simple terms and let them know, for example, how you handle customers who aren't very happy or what you do to make sure they return.

WHAT YOUR CHILD IS LEARNING

At the heart of the sales process there should be an understanding of value and of teamwork. We can only 'sell' something to someone if we understand that person's wants and motivation, then seek to satisfy those wants in a win-win situation.

Entrepreneurs do not 'sell' to passive recipients of their sales techniques, rather they engage their customers in a co-operative dialogue to help them perceive and satisfy the customer. needs. Only in doing this will they be successful - where success is measured always in terms of customer satisfaction and real value for both parties.

In these activities you are introducing your child to the world of trade, helping them to become familiar with both the processes and also the underlying principles such as the exchange of value, mutual benefit, customer service, and customer satisfaction.

The art of storytelling

Through the process of writing this book and in particular carrying out the interviews for it, many stories have been told – stories of young people achieving against the odds, of entrepreneurs striking out, and of family values influencing big decisions. For centuries, storytelling has played an important part in everyday life, and still does. The business world is no different. Many business leaders and entrepreneurs use storytelling to inspire their teams, or to encourage others to take action.

Children naturally love to hear stories, and it's good to encourage them to create and share their own, whether that's talking about what happened at school or making up their own as part of a game. Storytelling is also great for stimulating children's imagination as well as supporting the development of communication skills.

ACTIVITIES

Tell it your way

Help your child become the storyteller with an e-reader app. There's a good chance at least one smartphone in your household has already been taken over by your 4+ year old swiping, tapping, and sighing their way through *Angry Birds*, *Tiny Wings*, or any other games you finally gave in to and downloaded.

The good news is there are also a number of excellent e-reader apps for use on smartphones for younger children who are just learning to read or becoming more confident readers. Apps such as the *Ladybird Classic me Books*[17] shortlisted in the app category of the 2012 Guardian Digital Innovation Awards[18] are very popular with children in this age range as they can either have a go at reading the words or simply click on the pictures and tell the story

[17] http://itunes.apple.com/gb/app/ladybird-classic-me-books/id453238220?mt=8
[18] http://www.guardian.co.uk/megas/shortlist1

in their own words, whether that's *Little Red Hen* or *Peppa Pig*. The Enterprising Child web site[19] has a list of particularly good e-reader apps for children of this age.

Writing

As children of this age learn to form letters and write, you can build activity through encouraging them to write their own story book. It doesn't have to be a long story and can include pictures your child has either drawn or printed from the web (always check copyright). There are usually regular competitions from companies such as the *Tesco Kids*[20] book club who currently run one for children ages 2-5 and 6-8, or you could take a theme such as the Nativity at Christmas and get them to tell the story in their own words and pictures.

If your child isn't keen on writing, then recording a story (video/voice) may work better. Try experimenting with a range of media to get a feel for what your child responds most positively to.

Recording

Summer holidays provide a great opportunity to get out and about, to try lots of new activities as your child's confidence and abilities develops, and to meet up with friends. Recording holiday time is a great way to help your child learn the art of storytelling. They could use a scrapbook and draw pictures, or use a digital or cheap disposable camera (depending on manual dexterity) to take photographs, and collect leaflets or souvenirs (e.g. a shell from the beach) from their visits/activities.

The process of collecting everything together towards the end of the holidays, putting them in chronological order and presenting them in the scrapbook provides an opportunity to not just reflect on what they did, but also learn more about ways to tell and present

[19]www.enterprisingchild.com
[20]http://kidsbookclub.tescomagazine.com/

stories. Plus, of course, you will have a wonderful record of holidays for when they're all grown up.

Speak out loud

Depending on your child's personality, they may or may not need any encouragement in this area. Through early primary school years they will be involved in some kind of 'sharing' or 'show and tell' time in class – an opportunity for children to tell their classmates what they've brought in to school, what they did over holidays and so on.

Wherever possible, encourage this kind of activity at home. Perhaps they've written something at school that could be shared with the rest of the family, or it may simply be sitting around the dinner table and talking about their day. There are lots of opportunities for you to model this behaviour and the more opportunities you give for your child to learn and practise speaking out loud the more their confidence will grow.

WHAT YOUR CHILD IS LEARNING

Storytelling is an excellent way to develop the foundations of teamwork. Through storytelling children learn about and take into account different perspectives and experiences, developing their 'theory of mind' further and enriching their experience of the inherently social nature of stories and their shared reality.

Through encouraging the creative use of imagination you are also, of course, developing your child's perception of possibilities and encouraging innovation and different ways of looking at things, which are essential entrepreneurial characteristics.

Money doesn't grow on trees – or does it?

'Learning the value of money' is a much used phrase, but what does it really mean and how does it relate to the development of entrepreneurial skills and attitudes? Learning about the value of money is inseparable from learning about the significance of money in our social life and relationships, both in the home and in the wider world.

The value of money is not to be understood just in terms of currency values (although at this age this too is essential), or as an excessive preoccupation with money as an end in itself – there is a whole world of difference between a banker and an entrepreneur – but through an appreciation of its role in social relationships i.e. earning, giving, sharing, and saving, leading ultimately to an understanding of the social and moral dimensions as well as the practical aspects of trade and enterprise.

ACTIVITIES
Now or later?
The dilemma of whether to buy an item now or later occurs on many occasions and will depend on different factors, not least how strong the desire is to buy and whether there are competing demands on finances.

At this age, your child is probably only going to experience one aspect of this dilemma, which is of course the desire for the item, but there are ways to deflect from this and teach them that there are occasions when delaying the purchase may be the better option.

If you're not able to buy the toy for your child because money is tight, try to resist the urge to respond with 'I can't afford it'. This can set up a negative association with money although, as evidenced by some of the young entrepreneur interviews, a lack of money in the household actually made them more determined not to be in the same position when they grew up. Encourage your child to think about ways in which they may be able to earn and save money to buy the item they want. There is, of course, a balance required between getting your child to think creatively about how they might save the money whilst not taking on worries about any financial difficulties there may be at home.

An alternative approach is demonstrated by *Kirsty Henshaw* when she was out with her then six year old son Jacob, who put his request for a new toy in the context of the wider world:

> *Around Christmas time last year we were in a large toy outlet and he wanted everything… but I told him because his birthday was so close that he could have just one small toy for around £3. He was disappointed, but then I reminded him about the children in Africa and other third world countries who are less fortunate than him, who have to walk miles just to find clean water. It isn't about making him feel guilty; it's about awareness if not understanding about others around us. He decided to put the £3 in a charity box instead of buying the toy.*
>
> **Kirsty Henshaw, mum to Jacob (6½)**

Delaying or even not making the purchases in this way will help your child begin to learn that there are differences between wanting something and needing something. Recognising these differences will make a significant impact on understanding more clearly why such decisions are made. It encourages prudence and enables them to differentiate between affordable and worthwhile investments and indiscriminate spending, and to delay gratification where required – an essential entrepreneurial trait.

Use cash

With so many debit and credit cards available and with an increasing number of outlets now accepting contactless methods of payment, it's likely children are growing up rarely seeing and handling cash. When you're out shopping with your child, try to make an effort to pay for transactions with cash and let them see and feel the actual money. If you're in a supermarket, let them help you use the self-service till, put the money in, and watch the screen as it is counted. In local shops, encourage your child to hand over the money to the shopkeeper and wait for the change and receipt. All these opportunities to actually handle money will help them to understand that there are real constraints upon what is affordable based on what you actually have (in your purse, pocket, bank account), and avoid the infantile fantasy of unlimited wish-fulfillment that credit can encourage.

What's that worth then?

Around the age of five or six, children often like to start helping out a little more around the house, for example sorting the washing, helping in the garden, or setting the table for tea. This is an ideal time to start to teach your child about the relationship between work and money if you decide you're going to pay them for helping with tasks. Don't be surprised, though, if they start to try to negotiate on the value of tasks, particular if you are also teaching them about saving (see below) and they have a target in mind.

It is important, even at this young age, to help your child begin to understand that not everyone has the same amount of money (or physical health, ability or shelter), so helping out should not always involve financial reward. It can be difficult for young children to understand the wider world context so one approach might be to buy something with the money they would have earned from, say, washing the car, to give to a charity. Discuss with them different types of charities and let them choose which one they would like to donate to. Tangible donations other than cash may help them understand the concept of social giving much better.

A cautionary note that almost certainly goes without saying: never let education about money get in the way of the most important lesson of all: that love is unconditional and comes without a price-tag!

Getting the measure of money

This activity involves playing a game to work out which type of money has the greatest value. For example, if your child held 10 lots of 10p pieces in one hand and a £5 note in the other, there's a good chance they will say the coins have more value simply because they are heavier. This is a good opportunity to discuss perceived as opposed to actual value, as you help them count the coins and perhaps begin to explore the ideas of trust and agreement that convey value upon bank notes and other types of 'paper money'.

There are some great resources online to help your child learn about money, its face value and carrying out financial transactions, such as Doorway Online[21]. The Enterprising Child web site[22] has more information.

Setting targets

Introducing the concept of saving money to your child at this age plays an important part in helping them to learn elements of financial responsibility. They don't need fancy piggy banks or toy cash machines; a simple clear jam jar can work just as well and allow your child to see the money being saved.

At this age, having patience can be a difficult lesson, so try to help them set small, achievable financial targets as you feel

[21]www.doorwayonline.org.uk/cashingin.html
[22]www.enterprisingchild.com

appropriate for your child, based on for example a new toy they would like or an activity they want to do such as a visit to the local adventure park. If your child is using a jam jar, get them to make a little label for it showing the target amount. Stay involved in the process, giving them praise for doing so well. Occasionally you may want to add to their savings with a little 'extra' to boost the funds and give them a nice surprise and some encouragement.

Once young children begin to understand the benefits of saving money, they are often keen to continue. As they get older you can develop this understanding further through the activities in six to nine, *Should I save or should I spend?*

WHAT YOUR CHILD IS LEARNING

The enterprising child learns that their parents' money is earned by effort because they start to learn about the concept of work through being able to purchase things that they value, or gifts for sharing, with the rewards they earn from their own efforts. Learning that money is for sharing as well as earning is important given the lack of money that blights the lives of too many of the world's children.

The goal of the entrepreneurial lifestyle is to understand the world of supply and demand and to work with it to achieve social value. For most of us, making money has an altruistic element starting with the desire to provide for our own family needs. Understanding the role of money in social relations; the human significance of economic actvitity provides a foundation for a widening circle of altruism as we perceive the social goods that can come from wealth creation and distribution, and harness ambition and resolve to realise those wider values.

Manufacturing

An ambition to make a difference through either innovation or changing the way current systems or products work can only be fulfilled by firstly having a good understanding of the basics of 'the way things work'. A child who likes to get involved in activities and be very 'hands on' can be encouraged to engage in creative pursuits that potentially encompass and encourage the whole range of entrepreneurial characteristics.

ACTIVITIES
In the Garden
Gardening can be a great way to show your child how from one tiny seed a whole plant can grow. Try to find seeds of food your child or other members of the family like then start the planting process. Encourage them to get messy with the compost and regularly look after the seedling by giving it water and plenty of light. They might like to measure the plant's growth with a height chart. The more involved they are in this, the more they will understand the sequence of events required to create the vegetable they like. You can make this activity even more fun by helping them create weird and wonderful creatures or objects[23] from their growing efforts such as a cress caterpillar or mini scarecrow.

Jigsaw puzzles
Jigsaw puzzles can be a great way to help your child understand how piecing items together can make a whole. Resist the temptation to help them unless frustration sets in. If you don't have any jigsaws to hand try baking a tray of biscuit cake then using a range of different cutter shapes to see whether they can piece everything back together again, or you can make your own simple

[23]Garden Crafts for Children, Dawn Isaac, 2012 ISBN 1908170255

jigsaws from pictures in magazines stuck to card and cut into shapes.

Get crafty

There is probably no better way for your child to begin to understand manufacturing than to start their very own production line! From greetings cards to decorated eggs; papier maché to painting stones, the choices are endless. Some favourite crafts for this age range can be found in the Usborne *Playtime activities* book[24]

Emily aged 4 in her granddad's shed. Reproduced with kind permission from Emily Cummins.

If it can't be fixed – explore

It's a fact that at some point in the life span of children's toys, breakdowns happen. If it looks terminal, you could throw it out with the rubbish or at best attempt to recycle. An alternative which encourages your child to think about what makes a toy work (particularly one with electronic parts) is to open it up and explore.

There may not be much to see, and of course caution is required, but giving your child the opportunity to look inside the toy, view the component parts, and get an idea about how it worked will stimulate their interest in understanding how things are made.

Emily Cummins, a young British inventor recalls spending many hours with her granddad helping him to make and fix things.

At such a young age I was able to experiment and explore, he ignited my creative spark which is something I will always carry with me.

[24]Usborne Playtime activities, Ray Gibson, 1998 ISBN 0 7460 3340 0

Make something out of (almost) nothing

A great activity to help children of all ages learn about manufacturing, junk modeling encourages your child to make creative use of items you would otherwise have thrown away or recycled. Provide a range of items, textures, shapes and sizes from egg boxes to milk bottles, cardboard boxes to sweet wrappers and anything-else safe for them to use.

It's important, even at this age, to find a way for your child to record the process they're going to use to create their model. Possible methods are a simple design sheet[25] indicating what they need and what it will look like, to you translating the conversation into a list or mind map of ideas.

Don't forget that when the junk model has been made ask your child to *tell you* all about it rather than asking *'What's that, then?'* Invite them to talk through the manufacturing process and why it looks like it does. The more your child creates their own designs in this way and completes tasks such as cutting, sticking, and painting, the more they will grow in confidence about what they are capable of when it comes to ideas and innovation.

We're going on a berry hunt

If you happen to be out walking with your child during the blackberry or elderberry season, be sure to take a small container and collect a few handfuls of these fruits, making sure you leave enough for the birds and insects of course. You could simply go home, wash and cook them or you could try making small pots of inks using a simple three step process[26]. You could also use them as natural dyes with which to make printed t- shirts[27].

---

[25]See Enterprising Child website for design sheet template
[26]See Enterprising Child website for further details on how to make Inks or Dyes
[27]For more information read http://www.pioneerthinking.com/crafts/crafts-basics/naturaldyes.html

WHAT YOUR CHILD IS LEARNING

Despite its continuing decline, manufacturing remains the third largest sector in the UK economy in terms of share of UK Gross Domestic Product (GDP) and in 2009 representing just over 11% of the UK economy. It also employed around 2.6 million people, representing over 8% of the UK workforce.

Making stuff, and making better stuff, is a fundamental human activity, and our most basic economic process. A child whose imagination is captured by the creative impulse that lies at the heart of all manufacturing learns to perceive the possible hidden within the actual, the potential for change and innovation and, from their ambition to realise their vision, they discover depths of resolve within themselves. They frequently need to engage with others to achieve their goals, thus encouraging teamwork and learning the satisfaction that comes from creating something of value.

Giving it back

Entrepreneurial activity is concerned with the realisation of value, the production of goods and services that meet a need, the creation of jobs, the creation and distribution of wealth and providing the engine for cultural advancement. As such, entrepreneurial activity is a social phenomenon with an intrinsically ethical dimension – indeed some entrepreneurs like to make this realisation of social goods their primary focus, hence the rise of the *Social Entrepreneur*.

The activities here suggest ideas for developing in children this important altruistic and ethical core within the context of developing their entrepreneurial potential.

ACTIVITIES

Donating

Until now you've probably sorted out your child's toys without their help, either throwing away, donating to charity or friends, or selling. Now they're a little older, give your child the opportunity (Christmas and birthdays are good times) to sort out their toys and create different piles – one for charity, one for throwing away and so on. Explain to them the importance of keeping the *throw away* pile to a minimum – thinking environmentally, but also in value terms, one person's rubbish being another's treasure – and help them work out what toys could be mended or cleaned and then be given to charity.

Another activity is to find out what local charities operate around Christmas time to support, for example, struggling families. There are often calls for donations of clothes and toys for children so even if your child doesn't want to part with anything of theirs, you could take them shopping to choose a toy or an item of clothing to donate. If this is a regular call-out for help from the charity, then link this activity up with the savings one from *Money doesn't grow on trees – or does it?* and encourage them to set a target which will enable them to buy a new toy for someone less fortunate.

Fundraising – watch, learn, participate
Raising funds for charity is very popular and can range from the charity collection tins in shops –you can play a game and guess how many they can spot in one shopping trip – to the hilarious (sitting in a bath of cold baked beans) or adventurous (climbing up Kilimanjaro). If friends and family are engaged in fundraising activities, encourage your child to watch so they can see just how much fun helping others can be.

If they are inspired to do their own thing, help them decide which charity they want to support, with planning and getting sponsorship. The important thing is to make sure they understand why they're doing it and that it's lots of fun. They might also receive a certificate acknowledging the funds they've raised which can add to the delight, as in this example:

For the last three years my son has supported the Wallace and Gromit's Children's Foundation charity[28]. We've organised a tea party and he's completed a cycle ride. He appeared in the local press and was interviewed by a local radio station, which was a great experience for him.

Not long after his fifth birthday he decided to have a 'bake sale', creating a 'menu' and selling the cakes to local residents. He learned so much from this – planning how many cakes to make, how much to charge, how to present the cakes, and how to look after his customers by making sure they had a free sticker and tea bag. The charity was so inspired by his efforts they made him Fundraiser of the Month. He's now planning this year's activities

[28]www.wallaceandgromitfoundation.org

and as each year passes he understands more about the work of the charity and how he can make a difference to others.

Chris, dad to Dylan (5½)

Create to sell

Making products to sell and raise funds for charity can be a fun way to get involved and do something that your child really enjoys. If their interest is baking, help them hold a bake sale (with friends and family) – they'll be doing something they love and helping others at the same time, as well, of course, as learning those business skills of working out stock required, presentation, customer interaction, and counting money.

If painting or drawing is more their thing, putting on an art sale can work well, or for keen young gardeners growing plants from seeds and selling them is a great way for them to see how the activity they love can help others.

Your work

If you participate in voluntary activities, take time to talk with your child about why you are involved and what difference you feel it makes. If your place of work supports certain charities, explain why those particular ones were chosen and show them leaflets/videos/photographs of who the support is helping.

WHAT YOUR CHILD IS LEARNING

The most significant thing a child can learn from these kinds of activities is that others have needs and that life is not always fair in the distribution of opportunities and resources. They also learn that they can *make a difference* and that putting in effort to help others can bring a great sense of reward.

We hope that this core realisation will stay with children as they grow and develop, and provide an ongoing incentive to realising value and overcoming obstacles with compassion and a creative approach to social problems as a cornerstone of their entrepreneurial character.

Interview with Kirsty Henshaw, founder of *Kirsty's* and *Dragons' Den* winner

KIRSTY HENSHAW is founder of *Kirsty's* and mum to Jacob age 6½. Kirsty is known to many as the young woman who entered the *Dragons' Den* in 2010, taming Peter Jones and Duncan Bannatyne who between them invested £65,000 in her business, then named *Worthenshaws* – a company producing allergen free, nutritious frozen desserts developed as a result of her own son's food allergies.

Kirsty was born in Preston, Lancashire and brought up by her mum and step-dad (her real father didn't play a part in her life), Nanna and Granddad.

TELL US A LITTLE ABOUT YOUR FAMILY BACKGROUND AND HOW YOU FEEL YOUR MUM IN PARTICULAR INFLUENCED YOUR DECISIONS ABOUT WORK AND BUSINESS

'The first thing to say is that my upbringing was not a privileged one. I lived in an area of high unemployment where most of the neighbours were living on benefits,' says Kirsty when asked about her childhood. She recalls, however, that her family was different to many of the ones around her in that her mum worked very long hours and because of that her main carers were Nanna and Granddad and later on her step-dad (her mum re-married when Kirsty was seven).

'Mum worked shifts and put herself through a nursing degree, she

progressed through the nursing ranks, but as a child I just remember her working a lot. I also remember wondering why it was that we had no money even though she worked all those hours,' reflects Kirsty, answering the question herself with the fact that times were hard and her mum earned little more than what she would have been given in benefits. Lack of money meant that what few holidays they did have were fairly basic (camping/walking) but she also learned that the underlying values of living a good and happy life were more important to her family than earning a lot of money.

Her mum's strong work ethic is clearly something which has stayed with Kirsty through her 26 years, not least when she was holding down two part-time jobs and looking after Jacob as a single mum to save for the business she wanted. Kirsty does, however, remain staunchly unmaterialistic –*'I'm not at all materialistic,'* she laughs, *'after all, I'm dating a student.'*

That lack of money in her childhood, however, has made her determined not to be in the same position.

'I remember thinking I'm going to earn good money when I get older,' says Kirsty, and whilst she currently takes just a small salary from the still growing business, the potential future and lifestyle it offers is what's keeping her in business rather than being an employee.

'I'm impatient for it,' (the wealthy lifestyle) she says, but then with a dose of realism adds, *'but I'm in it for the long term.'*

Since her nursing career ended her mum has set up a natural healthy living business which has enabled Kirsty to learn plenty about issues such as accessing distribution chains. Her mum's response to Kirsty deciding to grow the business through Dragons' Den investment was mixed.

'She loved the product, but was horrified at the thought of me selling to the big supermarkets. She said to me 'You can't do that, the small health food producers won't like you,' but that was where Mum and I differed – I was thinking Big,' laughs Kirsty.

*'The first two years of running the business I was working at night
when Jacob had gone to sleep. Since then I have been with Adam (the
student) so Jacob spends quite a bit of time with him whilst I'm
working in the day and when he's not at school.'*

Kirsty takes time to reflect on how she feels her business is
impacting on Jacob.

*'He understands why I'm working (in his words 'so we can have nice
things') but doesn't always know why I don't come home from the office
until late.'* (Recently he had called her asking, 'Why won't you come
home?') *'I think he resents it a bit and tells me I'm boring when at the
weekends I'm trying to fit so much in, and he prefers to spend time with
Adam who's a lot more fun.'* When asked how that makes her feel,
Kirsty pauses, then replies, *'I'm feeling sad because we're not as strong
as we could be and he's still too young to really understand what I'm
doing all this for, but in the Summer we go for a walk every evening
together and we talk about work if he's interested, although usually
neither he nor Adam are and, to be honest, I have a great mentor I speak
with regularly so I don't have a great need to talk about it all at home.
Jacob and I chat all the time and he's a bright young boy.'*

Kirsty believes that her mother's strong work ethic has rubbed
off on her and her own is now doing the same with Jacob. *'He
definitely wants to work and earn money, although not in his own
business,'* she says. *'The other day I said to him 'You might want to
run Mummy's business in the future,' but he replied very strongly with
a clear No!'*

Kirsty gives some great examples of activities she does with
Jacob to encourage him to learn some of the really important skills
and characteristics for his future career, whatever that may be. For
example, he has his own bank account which they regularly check
online together. *'He has developed a strong save rather than spend*

approach to money and is quickly learning the value of everyday things such as Sky TV and the food shopping,' she says. *'I never say we haven't got the money, that's so negative. I learned as a child, and I am teaching him, that there are so many things in life which can be enjoyed that don't cost money.'*

As each birthday approaches, Kirsty and Jacob sort through his toys and decide what to take to charity and what to sell on eBay. They do the selling and dispatch together, and any money made is put into his bank account. *'Around Christmas time last year we were in a large toy outlet and he wanted everything,'* said Kirsty, *'but I told him because his birthday was so close that he could have just one small toy for around £3. He was disappointed, but then I reminded him about the children in Africa and other third world countries who are less fortunate than him, who have to walk miles just to find clean water. It isn't about making him feel guilty; it's about awareness of others around us.'*

As I was curious to know the outcome, Kirsty completed the story *'He decided to put the £3 in a charity box instead of buying the toy,'* she smiles. That's a great example of awareness leading to understanding which in turn may lead to better decision making — all from a 6½ year old.

When asked what she wishes the most for Jacob, Kirsty replies, *'Most of all I want to mould Jacob into a great human being.'*

WHAT TIPS CAN YOU GIVE TO PARENTS READING THIS BOOK?
'Let them learn and make their own mistakes. Allow them to be entrepreneurial and to think for themselves.

'Set enough boundaries to keep them safe. When they get older, don't pick up the pieces — they need to learn the art of self-sufficiency.

'Help them learn the value of money at a young age. Don't let them have whatever they want, this creates complacency and they don't understand about having to work for things.'

Kirsty admits she takes a very informal, flexible approach to parenting, which may reflect the fact that she was a single parent in Jacob's early years. Her final words on the subject? *'Working hard and being a single parent is hard work, really hard, but your children will remember that, and they will be incredibly proud.'*

Activities for children aged 6-9 years

Let me entertain you

Should I save or should I spend?

Giving it back

Destination decision

Manufacturing

Rate the sale

Let's get physical

The games children play

Minding my own business

Let me entertain you

As we have already mentioned, storytelling plays an important role in work and business as managers, educators, advertisers, entrepreneurs and business leaders use it to inspire and motivate others. Exposing your child to a wide range of stories through mixed media such as music, television, games console or books can help them learn more about the world they live in. They are learning about the diversity of human experience and understanding and also about our common humanity, through engaging with their own and others' stories.

It's important to help children learn that stories can have an impact on the way they think and feel; that stories can reframe experiences and be powerful motivators; that the stories we tell and hear can shape our own experiences – but most importantly that we can make up our own stories and don't have to just uncritically accept the stories we are told.

ACTIVITIES

Write it, read it, tell it how it is through mime
As your child develops more confidence in forming letters and writing, encourage them to start their own story book. It doesn't have to be long and can include pictures either your child has drawn, or which are printed from the web (don't forget to check copyright if it's going to be used for anything other than personal use).

There are often regular competitions such as the *Tesco Kids Book Club*[29] for children aged 6-8 or you could take a theme such as the Nativity at Christmas and get them to tell the story in their own words.

If your child isn't keen on writing, explore with them other ways of storytelling, such as dressing up, rhyming, oral storytelling such as recording stories on audio, video or smartphone, collecting and

[29]http://kidsbookclub.tescomagazine.com/story-competition.html

arranging photographs or cutting out pictures, drawing stories and so on. Another area to explore is that of creative movement where stories are told through miming activities. Choose a theme which interests your child, for example pirates, and encourage their creative movements to cover areas such as miming the scrubbing of the ship's deck, looking out for other ships, searching for treasure on the beach, fighting the enemy. You could put some pirate style music on in the background too.

Recording/interviewing

Everyone has a story to tell and it's easy to lose whole chunks of family history when an elderly relative passes away. If your child has a close relationship with a grandparent, for example, encourage them to ask that person to tell stories of when they were growing up, going to school, or work, and get your child to record those memories on paper, audio or video. Putting some thought into the interviewing process will help your child to understand about narrative structure (that most stories have a beginning, middle and end, with an internal chronology) and emotional and social significance – what is it that makes certain aspects of a story interesting or important? This process will also help your child develop an understanding about concepts of time, such as past and present, in relation to particular events.

Let me entertain you

There are so many creative ways children can get involved in storytelling and setting up a puppet show can work well at this age. There are some small puppet show kits on sale or, if you're feeling ambitious, let them have a go at building their own using whatever resources you have around the home. As children's author *Priya Desai* said, *'Creativity lies within being able to make use of what you have around you.'*

Here is a great example one parent gave:

We recently bought a 'build your own puppet theatre' box. It cost £2 and although I wasn't sure whether it was something my five year old son would enjoy, I thought it might be worth a go. He had great fun assembling it then hunted around the house for anything that looked puppet-like. We managed to find a frog, a rabbit, and a singing kiwi bird! I have to admit I wasn't sure what kind of story could be made with that but my son created one and within a short time we ended up with a great five minute show called 'The frog and the missing kiwi'.

Now, every time we have visitors, he insists on putting on the little puppet show. Doing this hasn't just helped to develop his imaginative, creative, and storytelling skills, but built his confidence in entertaining others too.

Public performance

If you live near, or are visiting London with your child, take time to visit Speakers' Corner, opposite Marble Arch tube station.

Speakers' Corner has been described as 'the spiritual home of the British democratic tradition of soapbox oratory[30]' and most days, especially Sundays, you will find someone there with a story to tell, taking the opportunity to share their opinions, values, and beliefs. You never know who is going to be there so the content and quality may vary, but as an opportunity to experience some genuine rhetorical passion and argument it is invaluable. Street theatre is not that common outside major cities but it can be enthralling for a child.

Reviewing the story

Watching films or going to special events can provide a great opportunity for your child to get involved in re-telling the story of what happened either by writing or recording their thoughts.

[30]http://www.londontown.com/LondonInformation/Attraction/Speakers_Corner/4460/

The UK *Young Film Critic*[31] competition is open to any school pupil aged between 4 to 11 years old. Ages 4 to 7 are asked to submit a poster design based on a film they've seen recently and ages 7 to 11 are asked to submit a written and/or video review. This can only be entered via school, but there's no reason why, if your child is keen on watching and reviewing films, they can't send their review in to the local paper who might print it for other young readers.

All together now

Putting on a family play, reading stories, or playing games together can enable your child to learn about the way in which tone and expression are varied to get particular messages across. Be as creative as you like and if, for example, you're reading a book together, work with your child to determine which kind of voices go with particular characters and why.

A good game is to give each member of the family a card with a sentence and a note on how to read it e.g. angry, sad, embarrassed, then get other members of the family to guess the emotion being conveyed.

[31]http://www.youngfilmcritic.org/

WHAT YOUR CHILD IS LEARNING

Mastering the art of understanding and telling stories is a fundamental part of being human, indeed human culture can be defined in terms of the stories we tell about ourselves, so it has to be a very important part of any child's upbringing. More than this, the greater the mastery of the art of storytelling the greater our understanding of ourselves and others, which is essential to the leadership, salesmanship and team building aspects of the entrepreneurial mindset. The more flexible and imaginative we can be in the art of storytelling, the more we can find new ways of looking at things and perceive possibilities that others may miss.

Should I save or should I spend?

"It's wonderful to see our son realising for himself the value of money. The other day Iolo had some change from the shop. He handed it to his dad and said, "Here, Dad, you'll need this for building the house." It was only two pence but it shows that he is understanding that things cost money."

Jasmine, mum to Iolo (6) and Rufus (2 ½)

Developing a basic level of understanding about money in terms of both its face value and the price of everyday items is a good basis from which to begin teaching your child about financial responsibility. You can begin to teach your child about important areas such as budgeting, setting targets, and cash flow (don't panic!) which anyone working in or for a business will need an understanding of.

If your child seems to have a genuine interest in and ability for mathematics then build on that by expanding these suggested activities as you feel appropriate, otherwise just introduce the subjects naturally and gently through the course of the activities. Many business people will be the first to admit that 'numbers' are not their forte, which is why there are helpful people called accountants, but all will agree on the importance of understanding at least the basics of finance.

ACTIVITIES

Shopping trips

At this age, children become more aware that there is a price tag attached to not just new toys, but also household items. Take opportunities as they arise to teach your child about prices of everyday and special purchases when you're out and about. Encourage them to start looking at prices, noticing, for example, the price differences between 'branded' and 'value' items.

Going somewhere nice? Let's budget!

When you're next planning a trip out, involve your child in making decisions about how much money to take by discussing what you may need to pay for. There may be parking charges, entrance fees, raffle tickets or ice-creams at a summer fair or adventure park. Make a list of potential expenditures with your child and agree on the budget to keep within. Here's how one dad teaches his child about financial responsibility and budgeting:

> *We have a favourite play park and zoo near us where the costs can really mount up – entrance fees, charges for fairground rides and ice-creams. I agree in advance with my six year old how many rides he can go on and whether or not we will have an ice-cream. This involvement means a more financially manageable outing for me and my son learns about the costs associated with trips and how to keep to a budget.*

This approach to involving your child in planning an outing begins to teach them about the basic principles of budgeting and encourages the use of some basic maths skills.

Get a handle on cash

As mentioned earlier, the increasing use of plastic (debit or credit) cards means there are fewer opportunities for your child to see and feel cash, so it's important that you give them as many opportunities as possible to handle money and complete financial transactions. The more your child becomes familiar with physical cash, the better they will understand the reality of money, for example that an item costs four weeks' pocket money, instead of being dazzled by the apparent instant availability of money that credit card use suggests. There is a significant difference between handing over money from your purse or piggy bank and clicking on-line to buy something via a credit card.

Many children have not visited a bank, particularly as online banking is so popular, so it's worthwhile making the effort to occasionally take them to your local bank to show them how you operate your own account and see others visiting the bank to hand over cash, pay in cheques, withdraw money and so on.

Savings and Targets

Whether it's making[32] or buying a money box, opening a child's savings account or using a spare pot in the house, take time to show your child the importance of saving money not just for its own sake but for a purpose. It's generally a good idea at this age to set relatively small, easily achievable targets, increasing in size and difficulty as they progress.

There are plenty of options available which allow children to see how much money they're saving at any one time. Many of the manufactured toys use similar technology to vending machines which allow your child to put in coins and even notes. They then set a target amount of money to save, a set number of days they think it will take to reach the target, then save regularly (perhaps from helping out with chores around the house) either with or without making the occasional withdrawal of funds.

The process of setting a target, earning money to achieve it and understanding how spending will delay the achievement of that target forms a sound base for understanding about the world of work and business.

As your child becomes more familiar with the process of saving, start to bring it into everyday situations such as when they see a new game they'd like: set the target (cost of the game) and discuss ways in which they can begin to earn money to save for it. Bear in mind, however, that this is still a fairly young age so only use it

[32]Papier mache link - http://www.ehow.co.uk/how_2132130_paper-mache-piggy-bank.html

where it feels appropriate and remember to set relatively small, easily achievable targets as patience and interest can still be very limited.

The gift of money

Birthdays and Christmas are popular times for children to be given money, so take these opportunities to discuss with your child whether they plan to save or spend it, or a combination of both. They're probably not going to be able to completely understand the reality of the face value of money above, say, £10 or £15 so you many want to break it down into small, more easily understandable amounts then help them decide how much to spend and how much to save. It's tempting to just hold on to the money for them and bring it out as and when there is a toy they'd like or for an extra trip out somewhere, but try to resist that and remember that trusting them to manage this money will help them understand and take financial responsibility.

A gift for others

Many children of this age will enjoy being involved in shopping for birthday gifts for close family members or friends, so the next time they're invited to a party let them follow the whole process through, from deciding what to buy their friend, making sure there is enough money available and allowing them to pay for the item by withdrawing the money from the account or piggy bank and paying the shopkeeper themselves.

Budgets

Known to cause fear in even the most savvy of business people, the idea of introducing budgets and perhaps cash flow forecasting to your child at this age probably sounds at best unrealistic and at worst a recipe for disaster, but towards the latter end of this age range your child could get involved in several areas which introduce the concept of budgeting.

At its most straight forward, a budget is simply a way of working out how much money is coming in, how much is going out and what the money is being spent on over a period of time. If your child has already had a go at the savings and targets activity then they're half way to understanding budgets.

For older children, try involving them in some basics of household budgeting such as food and petrol. Tell your child what your weekly budget is for food and fuel then help them draw up a chart of planned expenditure for the month. If they're already familiar with spread sheets such as Excel through school they might enjoy recording the information in this way. Every time money is spent on food and fuel a note is made on a piece of paper from which your child can record actual expenditure against the budget. At the end of the month they will be able to see how well the family have kept within budget for food and fuel.

I like to sit and explain reasons why we have to do certain things with my children, especially Sophie, rather than just coming out with the usual rushed 'because I said so'. Sophie at four is really starting to understand things better now and we can talk about decisions concerning money. For example the other day she wanted to go on a bouncy castle but I had already planned for us to visit the Science Centre. We discussed the options and the money involved and she decided she'd stick with the Science Centre.

Cheryl Ryder, mum to Sophie (4), Craig (2½), Callum (1½)

Your work

If you run your own business, talk with your child about how you manage the money. Do you regularly pay cheques and/or cash into your bank or are transactions completed online?

It's probably a little early to start showing them your company spreadsheets or accounting software but talking with your child about keeping records, for example setting targets on expected sales forecasts, will help to develop their understanding about the role that managing money has to play in business.

> *'We talk quite a lot about my work, we go to the bank to pay money in, and perhaps when they're older they can spend a bit more time with me in the office if they're interested.'*
>
> **Claire Meredith, Mum to Dylan (5) and Lloyd (2)**

WHAT YOUR CHILD IS LEARNING

The social significance of money, the acquisition of concepts such as *earning, sharing, deserving, giving,* and *saving* that began in the 4-6 years stage continues to develop here, but increased cognitive and mathematical skills also enable children to focus with more realism on the mechanics of money handling. Underlying this practical skillset, however, is the need to develop not only an appreciation of what is 'real', but also of what can be (the perception of possibility) and what is of value.

The expression about someone 'knowing the price of everything and the value of nothing' is the opposite of what is being developed in the enterprising child. While discovering things of value within their world, they also learn to master their own impulses, to defer immediate gratification for longer term value – a key entrepreneurial characteristic.

Giving it back

In a world often preoccupied with commercial gain it would be easy to overlook the fact that there is a moral and social framework within which children must be educated – touched upon in the Giving it back age 4-6 years section. Helping children understand that the world is not equal in terms of access to shelter, healthcare, finance, education, environment and much more introduces them to the moral and social impact of economic activity.

Giving something back to society, whether by volunteering, solving problems through innovation, fundraising, or donating money, means recognising the value inherent in all human life, the earth and all its creatures. It means acknowledging that our own gifts carry responsibilities and that we are not here just to pursue our private wellbeing.

Giving your child opportunities to get involved in activities with social value also helps them to benefit from developing entrepreneurial skills and the experience of seeking creative ways to benefit others. It fulfils a fundamental duty of parents to bring up rounded, responsible, ethical citizens.

ACTIVITIES

Inspired by others

Harry Moseley. *Reproduced with kind permission from Georgina Moseley*

Being inspired by others is often what leads people to get involved in charity fundraising or helping out in the first place, and there is no better example of this in young people than Harry Moseley – a very special boy who lived in Sheldon, UK.

At seven years of age Harry was diagnosed with a brain tumor and whilst in hospital receiving treatment he met someone going through the same thing, which inspired Harry to start making and selling beaded bracelets to raise money for Brain Cancer Research.

Just four weeks into the campaign, Harry's friend passed away, but Harry continued with both his own battle with cancer and his campaign. As well as selling the bracelets, Harry got involved in visiting schools and businesses talking about his work and raised hundreds of thousands of pounds for the charity

Sadly, in October 2011 aged just 11 years old, Harry died, but what he achieved in his short life time remains an inspiration for children and adults alike. You and your child can find out more about Harry's story and support his campaign[33] and, who knows, it might inspire your child to do something to help others too.

Solution focused

A child brought up to recognise that there are problems in the world, but not over-exposed to the injustices (which can be age inappropriate) can, with support, find opportunities to engage in altruistic efforts to help charities resolve problems. By doing so they will have a more effective and positive approach to the world's ills. A child encouraged to merge their concern for others with their developing entrepreneurial characteristics and a creative can do approach has the makings of a successful social entrepreneur, someone intent on finding and implementing solutions that will make the world a better place.

Simple, solution focused tasks at home could be introduced through, for example, noting that when the light goes out a replacement light bulb or fuse will provide the solution to the problem.

[33]www.hhho.co.uk

Although a little older than the age range covered here, young British inventor *Emily Cummins* created a solution to a problem when she realised one of her grandfathers was having difficulty using the toothpaste tube because of his arthritic hands. From inventing a toothpaste dispenser her grandfather could use, she went on to build a water carrier to help African women and children who often have to walk many miles to collect water and then a sustainable refrigerator which is now used across Southern Africa, and improves the quality the lives of both the women who are creating them and the people who use them. In Emily's words:

> *...when I realised I could help people with my products, they became even more important and I wanted them to be the very best they possibly could.*

Diversity

Learning more about the world we live in and its inequality is an important lesson as your child journeys through their life. The use of the word *journeys* here is deliberate as adventures, whether on the bus, train or on foot, can provide excellent opportunities for your child to learn more about the diverse world they live in.

The next time you're on a journey with your child, whether it's simply going to school or a longer journey, try playing the *Who? Where? Why?* game. Encourage your child to look around at the people they pass on the journey and guess 'who' the person is workwise, based on the clothes they are wearing, anything they're carrying or what they're doing. Next, guess 'where' they are (on their way to work, to the dentists, to visit a friend). How much can your child tell (or make judgments) based on what they can see, from purposeful walks to facial expression?

Finally, 'why' does your child think the person has chosen that particular mode of transport? Do they live a long way from work, can't cycle or don't have a cycle helmet, or does the bus timetable not fit in with their requirements?

By people watching – looking at clothes, expressions and environment – your child is beginning to notice and respect differences in the world, and to develop theories of motivation that will enhance their capacity for social understanding and empathy.

Your work
If you participate in voluntary activities, take time to talk with your child about why you are involved and what difference you feel it makes. If you run a business and support certain charities, explain why you chose those particular ones, show them leaflets/videos/ photographs if appropriate of who your activities are helping.

WHAT YOUR CHILD IS LEARNING
In this section we have been concerned with the development of entrepreneurial characteristics such as imagination, ambition, the capacity to accept and manage risk, the resolve to see things through, and working with others, but above all it is about being creators of value and not just passive consumers. In short, we are encouraging children to begin to use imagination and curiosity to address real social problems and become compassionate agents for change. That experience and understanding of giving will develop a child's comprehension of the elements of social entrepreneurship and giving something back to society.

Destination decision

Problem solving through decision making is a crucial part of everyday life in work or at home; at this age children are becoming more independent, so providing opportunities for them to take responsibility when decision making can help develop their confidence, self-esteem and, of course, problem solving and decision making skills.

Many of the young entrepreneurs interviewed here commented on how their parents' work ethic played a significant part in decisions they went on to make about work and business. This is not surprising as decision making is always based on a personal narrative rooted in childhood influence.

As well as providing opportunities for children to be involved in decision making, parents should model effective and rational decision making: talking to your child or even yourself as you consider the best course of action, provides your child with a model of reasoned deliberation they can then internalise.

ACTIVITIES

Transportation

Noticing the different types of transport people use can stimulate discussion with your child as seen in the *Diversity* activity in *Giving it back*. For example, why do some people drive instead of taking the bus or train; or choose to fly on holiday rather than go by boat?

If your child considers their own journey from home to school and back, it may involve little independent decision making. For example, they might live in a rural area with limited public transport and no safe pavements for walking, so a car may be the only option. For others, though, perhaps the issue is about the *time* it takes to get to school and the distance involved, which means a quicker means of transport is necessary.

Encourage your child to work out all the different types of transport (including walking or cycling) possible to get from their home to school and try to work out how long it would take and the relative pros and cons of each option. A sample journey planning sheet is available on the Enterprising Child website[34].

Give a little

Giving your child the opportunity to practise independent decision making will help their confidence grow as well as to recognise where a problem may exist and possible solutions.

Exploring the process of decision making by breaking it into small steps will help your child focus on particular aspects, such as defining the problem, exploring pros and cons of choices, understanding consequences and reviewing the decision after it has been made. A very significant part of this process is to encourage the use of imagination and a sense of value, for example by asking 'How would you feel if...?' or 'What would be the best/worst thing that could happen if you did X rather than Y?'

> *I take time to talk and explore issues with them... It's about exploring actions and consequences. Sometimes Xander will say 'I wish x would happen' and we talk about that, about why it might not happen.*
>
> **Zoe Brown, mum to Naomi (21),**
> **Xander (7), Evan (5), Hollie (2), and Abie (1)**

Daily decisions

As your child matures they will need to make decisions more often, whether about going to a party, who to play with at the weekend or what to spend their pocket money on.

---

[34]www.enterprisingchild.com

Financial decision making can also come into play, particularly if you get them involved in the *Should I save or should I spend?* activity.

Decisions taken every day in family life show your child the importance of consensus where possible, fairness, and how they are often taken based on information available, e.g. decisions about going out may be dependent on weather information. Encourage your child to ask questions to help them make decisions.

The '*Planning*' activities require decisions to be made about which member of the family does what and when, as well as deciding what to eat on a particular day.

Now or later?
There are some great games you can play with your child or as a family to learn about good or bad decision making. Deciding whether to accept money now or later is particularly fun when faced with the *double a penny* dilemma that has been around a long time and is suitable for children at the higher end of this age category. Give your child the choice to (hypothetically) accept being given a penny a day and have it doubled every day after that for 29 days, or to receive £1 million pounds immediately.

The results are fascinating – you'll need to log on to the Enterprising Child website to find out if you don't already know them.

Whatever game you decide to play, take the time afterwards to talk about why family members made the decision they did: what information did they use; verbal or non-verbal cues? Discuss whether they might do something different next time around.

WHAT YOUR CHILD IS LEARNING

The entrepreneurial character is one that recognises possibilities and ambitiously seeks to realise value through managed risk. Obviously good decision making can make the difference between success and failure in seeking to realise goals. The enterprising child learns to make and justify their own decisions, not to be led by the crowd or conform to peer pressure and for that they need an early introduction to the process of reasoned decision making so that they develop confidence, but also a respect for what they can learn from others and the environment, and the ability to recognise, adapt, and remain resilient and flexible in the face of negative or unforeseen consequences to their decisions.

Manufacturing

Moving on from the creative involvement in making things as seen in earlier years, these activities focus on learning more about the process of production, about identifying and using resources to produce something of value.

ACTIVITIES

Gate to plate – back to basics

Most children of this age know that milk comes from a cow, but they may be less sure about the provenance of other basic items such as yoghurt or cheese. In a recent survey[35] by the farming charity Leaf[36] it was revealed that less than half of young adults know that butter comes from a dairy cow, with a third unaware that eggs are laid by hens. Whilst this survey focused on 16-23 year olds, an earlier one five years ago[37] of 1,000 children aged 8-15 also revealed far less understanding about where such produce came from. It's not just important because informed consumers, as we know, make better and healthier choices, but because an alienation from the process of production makes it harder to see the creative possibilities and so closes off a whole area of possible entrepreneurial engagement.

One way to make sure your child not only knows where basic food stuff comes from, but also learns about the processes necessary for it to reach the kitchen table, is to visit a local farm. Talking with the farmer (perhaps at a farmers' market if you can't get to a local farm) about how their bread/milk/meat/preserved

[35]http://www.dailymail.co.uk/news/article-2159174/LEAF-survey-One-young-adults-think-eggs-come-wheat.html
[36]www.leafuk.org
[37]http://menmedia.co.uk/manchestereveningnews/news/education/s/1000/1000505_city_kids_think_cows_lay_eggs.html

products are made will help make the whole process of food production more tangible and personal for your child.

If you are able to visit a creamery or watch the cows being milked, talk with your child afterwards about the machinery or environment (noisy, messy) and encourage them to record the process in whichever way they prefer – photographs, video, writing.

The natural way

Your child can create their own manufacturing line right at home using simple, natural ingredients. From collecting blackberries or elderberries to using tea bags or fresh ground coffee, a simple process can be followed which results in superb looking dyed t-shirts or other fabric. They can also make natural inks from berries such as blackcurrants, blackberries, or raspberries[38].

If you don't have any of these ingredients to hand, fabric paints are a suitable alternative. Just cut out shapes in whatever fruit and vegetables you happen to have around, dip them in fabric paint, then print onto the t-shirt, following the paint manufacturer's instructions to heat secure the design.

The alternative way

It is never too early to start teaching children about energy saving, particularly around the home, and understanding more about how energy is manufactured is a good place to start. *The Young People's Trust for the Environment*[39] aims to 'encourage young people's understanding of the environment and of the need for sustainability' and provides a free magazine for children and well-designed fact sheets covering many aspects of sustainable energy.

[38]For more information visit http://www.pioneerthinking.com/crafts/crafts-basics/naturaldyes.html
[39]http://www.ypte.org.uk/

When you're out and about with your child, get them to look out for alternative energy sources, such as wind turbines in fields or solar panels on roof tops. There are several hydro-electric visitor centres in the UK which welcome family visits, so if you happen to live or go on holiday near one they are well worth a visit to learn more in a hands on way about how this energy is made. You can also buy or make simple kits that demonstrate solar or wind energy production.

A mini allotment
Whatever size garden you have, even if just a windowsill, encourage your child to choose seeds, plant them and watch them grow. They can record what happens by drawing, taking photographs or creating a measuring chart to track growth and quality.

It's a hive of activity
Whether or not your child has grown their own little garden, there's a good chance they will see honey and bumble bees flying around on the look-out for suitable flowers from which to collect nectar. *The Young People's Trust for the Environment* offers a free leaflet[40] written especially for young children all about the honey bee and how it manufactures honeycombs – particularly helpful if your child is a fan of honey.

Can you fix (or build) it?
The next time you have a job to do around the house or out in the garden which requires fixing or building skills, get your child involved. Building and/or fixing is at the core of a manufacturing process and it is through watching and participating in these skills that children learn, become confident in and engaged by the creative processes involved, as well as developing their manual and cognitive skills in this area.

[40]http://www.ypte.org.uk/files/Yipp-bees.pdf

We're building a house at the moment and Iolo loves getting involved. He has his own toolbox and helps out with small jobs like moving timber and clearing up after a job is done.

I think it's good that he sees me doing lots of things in and around the house and garden, so it's natural for him to want to help."

Ben, dad to Iolo (6) and Rufus (2½)

WHAT YOUR CHILD IS LEARNING

In the earlier years activities we alluded to the fundamental role that manufacturing – making stuff, whether it be food, clothing, household items or advanced technology – plays in human culture and economic activity. At this later stage we are looking beyond a general encouragement of the creative towards the more analytical process of designing, producing, and developing. This shift in focus introduces children to specific areas of production, from vegetable growing to clothing to computers, in order to stimulate their imagination, improve their understanding and give them practical opportunities to play with and explore the creation, modification, improvement or repair of manufactured products.

Rate the sale

Building on the activities from earlier years, you can now start to give children a little more responsibility when it comes to everyday buying and selling activities. They can begin to learn more about the role of supply and demand and how advertising can support sales generation.

It's interesting to note during the activities which areas your child appears to be most comfortable with, for example are they happier with presentation as opposed to the actual customer interaction; are they a 'marketing' person or more of a 'sales' person? This may give you an insight into their relative strengths, weaknesses, and motivating factors.

At this age your child is also likely to show an interest in comparing their achievements to others, so introducing rating systems such as 'marks out of ten' for areas such as customer service is likely to generate a positive response and inspire them to try again or try harder.

ACTIVITIES
Benefits not features
The next time your child points excitedly at the latest scooter, bike, or DS game in the hope you'll buy it for them, try eliciting a more detailed response from them as to why they want it other than 'because it's cool'. Ask them to tell you the benefits rather than features of having that particular item (assuming you're happy to buy it or they have sufficient savings), for example if it's a scooter then saying it will keep them fit is a benefit as opposed to detailing a feature such as 'it's got nice handlebars'. Your child will also begin to learn the art of persuasion which, whilst this may be a little problematic at times for you as a parent, will undoubtedly serve them well.

A helpful way of explaining to your child the difference between benefits and features is to say that if you are trying to sell something to someone then you need to put yourself in their shoes and imagine (and of course persuade them) just how having a better widget will make their life more pleasurable, rather than just detailing the features of a better widget in the hope they will be impressed. You can apply this to objects they already own, ask them for instance, why they might advise a friend to buy a bike like theirs (it's got alloy wheels, for example, would be a feature; alloy wheels are light and make you got faster would be a benefit and therefore a convincing reason).

Buying opportunities

During and after the buying process, encourage your child to think about the way in which the seller interacts with them: How did it make them feel? How many marks out of 10 would they give for 'customer service'? If they respond with less than 9 or 10 ask them what they think would need to happen or improve for the full 10 marks to be awarded for great customer service?

When you're visiting a shop you particularly like, talk with your child about what in particular it is you like about it: customer service, pricing, environment, displays, and so on.

Make time to browse

Schedule in a little extra time for browsing on your next shopping trip. Point out the differences between branded and value items as well as the various ways products are promoted (most shops will have promotional stalls or end of aisle offers). In shops as well as restaurants there are often 'specials' available: explore with your child why they think the items are being promoted as specials (for instance seasonal, or new product, near sell-by date, over-stocked).

Moving on to sales

As your child grows out of toys, help them have a sort out and consider either selling them at a car boot or garage sale or going online to one of the many auctions sites which are available.

Whichever you choose, encourage your child to look for similar toys being sold and consider issues such as quality (are the toys clean and in good condition), price including delivery costs (does the amount to be charged cover the costs of packaging as well as actual postage), and the description (otherwise known as the sales pitch) or in marketing speak the *value proposition*.

Farmers Markets

Farmers Markets have already been mentioned in several other activities as providing great opportunities for your child to learn about *Manufacturing* and *Selling it like it is*.

For this age range, the markets continue to be a great resource to stimulate entrepreneurial thinking in areas such as presentation, marketing, and advertising. Again, encourage your child to look at all the different displays and what kind of promotional materials are being used to attract attention, such as banners, leaflets, cooked products available for tasting before buying, and so on.

Who benefits from the sale?

There is, of course, more to completing a sale than meets the eye. Anyone in business will tell you that for products to reach consumers a whole series of processes and companies may be involved, from sourcing materials to manufacturers, and distributors. What is so good about sales? Well, they provide jobs and opportunities for all the people involved in bringing that product to market – no sales means no products and therefore no jobs. So, instead of complaining about those rather annoying sales people, you could explore their social value, tenacity and courage, for without selling there would be no enterprise, commercial or charitable. Ask your child questions such as 'Who do you think made this?' or 'Will the person who made this get all the money we've just paid them?' or 'How do you think these were transported to the shop?'

Your work

If your work involves any aspect of a sales process, including retail, manufacturing or distribution, take some time to talk with your child about how that works in the company. If you can, take them along to your place of work so they can see first-hand how products are made, moved or sold. If you work, or run a business in a service industry then the sales process will operate a little differently, with a focus on information materials, presentations, direct interaction with consumers, and often a negotiation process before services can be delivered and the sales process is complete. It can be more difficult to show how this works to a child, but media such as videos can help.

Simon Jordan TV[41] has an interesting video where he asks his own young children what they think about the logos of some well-known brands and what they associate with those brands. This is really interesting to watch and a good way of seeing things through a child's eyes.

[41]http://gathermoreclients.com/simonjordantv/featured/small-business-simplify-your-offering/

WHAT YOUR CHILD IS LEARNING

Selling is a part of everyday life and involves understanding different wants and needs; it requires a willingness to accept and deal with risk, including the risk of rejection. Put simply, learning to sell is about understanding how to engage others in your ideas through good social interaction, great communication (listening and responding) and presenting yourself and your ideas positively.

Selling has for a long time considered to have negative associations with cold calling, door step double glazing sales people and so on, but as mentioned earlier, selling is at the heart of all successful enterprises. Effective selling requires empathy, imagination and resilience. The best kind of selling comes from belief in the benefits that the product (or service) will bring; it is the opposite of cynical manipulation, which is why good sales people are often surprisingly willing customers as well, they are natural *believers*.

Let's get physical

At this age children are generally becoming more physically able and show significant improvement in both their gross and fine motor skills, building their physical strength and abilities as well as learning to pay more attention to detail. There are many fun, physical activities which can be carried out at home or out and about which build on this development, help increase their confidence levels, and help your child learn and build on essential team working, collaboration, design and creative and imaginative skills.

ACTIVITIES

Den in the woods today

A den can, of course, be built at home as well as in the woods. Simple materials such as a spare bed sheet or a couple of blankets and some chairs or a table could work well. Be brave and let your child have the run of the furniture (unless it really is precious) to see how creative they can be.

If they are out in the garden or woods then the Eden Project in Cornwall has some great ideas for den building, including a video[42] with 'Den Commandments' and 'Safe play tips' for building outside dens.

The fun doesn't stop when the den has been built. Let your child and friends decide how they're going to use this newly created space; they may decide to use it for quiet reading, snack time, or playing games.

If you are able to observe your child whilst they're den building, notice what part they play alongside others: do they take the lead on finding materials and building, or do they prefer to organise others; do they think about how it looks or consider what the space is going to be used for?

[42]http://www.edenproject.com/blog/index.php/2011/06/how-to-build-your-own-den/

Camping

Taking your child camping, whether in the back garden, on the beach, or to a camp site is a great way to encourage their use of a range of essential entrepreneurial skills. As in the *Planning* activities, it's best to get your child involved in as much of the planning process as possible and encourage them to make decisions about, for example, what kind of clothes they need to take, equipment for cooking, and so on. When the tent is up, again involve them in keeping the space organised and encourage them to think creatively about how they can be self-sufficient.

Let's go fly a kite

Learning to fly a kite can be a tricky business, requiring reasonable levels of hand-eye coordination as well as plenty of clear space – i.e. no roads, overhead cables, or trees nearby. Your child will need to think about weather conditions (too windy or not enough wind will make kite flying difficult), and of course they need to be prepared for the fact that at least for the first few attempts, the kite doesn't reach the skies. Kite flying can be frustrating and requires considerable patience, but the combination of painstaking attention to detail on the ground and the soaring poetry in motion and escape from gravity represented by a kite in flight is not a bad metaphor for the entrepreneurial path.

The Way of the way

Martial Arts are popular with many children. If you are looking for activities which promote balance, mental and physical co-ordination and mental/spiritual skills for handling stress, practising patience and self-control then one of these is worth considering.

Pedal power

Apart from the health and ecological benefits of cycling, a child who travels into adulthood with a love of cycling will always relish the freedom of adventure, the joy of self-propelled travel and independence and, in the car dominated culture, will understand an outsider position – useful in the entrepreneurial life. Add to this the self- discipline and resilience that comes from hill climbing and travelling in all weathers and cycling may well appeal as an ideal activity for entrepreneurial character building.

Climb every mountain

Children are natural climbers; left to themselves they will scale trees, buildings, even cliffs if available. You could harness that natural exuberance in a safer way by their learning to climb properly through an outdoor adventure centre or club (most accept children from aged eight upwards). Climbing can teach many useful skills – planning, imagination and perception, mental control, confidence, team work, resilience, risk assessment and management.

WHAT YOUR CHILD IS LEARNING

Physical activity is a fantastic way to develop key entrepreneurial characteristics. Not all children of course are 'sporty' or competitive, and not all are able bodied, but any child will enjoy some level of physical activity and challenge if the right outlet is found for their natural exuberance.

The activities selected here share with the multitude of other activities possible, an ability to present challenges, to encourage imagination and engagement, ambition, and resolve, and many have a social dimension that will help to develop latent team working and team building capabilities. Many companies invest time and money in providing access to outdoor education and adventure activities in order to develop their employees' enterprising characteristics and abilities. However, unlike many senior executives, children generally do not need to be cajoled into fun and adventure – they just need to be given the opportunity.

The games children play

Creativity is easily encouraged and can be taught through everyday parenting, not just through painting or model-making, but through their play in general and how they learn to channel creativity and develop their view of the world.

Paul Lindley, dad to Ella (12) and Paddy (9)

Children learn through play. Much of this is, and should be, natural and spontaneous and requires little in the way of resources. As children grow older, formal games with prescribed rules and opportunities for competition and challenge become increasingly popular; the disciplines learned through the world of game playing can contribute effectively to the development of entrepreneurial character – encouraging children to look and consider carefully; to understand rules and recognise patterns; to perceive possibilities and work hard to realise those possibilities.

ACTIVITIES
Not board yet!
Many of the traditional board games familiar to adults have made a comeback over recent years with popular brands such as Monopoly, Risk, and Battleships proving to be firm family favourites. Some of these games (Monopoly is the obvious one but there are many more), have a 'business' framework which can help to encourage entrepreneurial behaviour, but all of them involve social interaction and understanding motivations, an element of 'deal making' and the need to formulate strategies and plans to succeed.

Chess (and Draughts for younger children) remain excellent resources for helping children understand patterns, and recognise and exploit possibilities.

Electronic Games

Whether it's on a computer, a games console or a mobile phone, the rise of electronic games has been perceived as a cause for concern, but, like most things in life, in moderation these games have their value (aside from keeping your children occupied when necessary), not least in terms of helping your child focus their attention for reasonable lengths of time. Most electronic games will also require your child to make decisions ranging from whether to, for example, turn right, turn left, jump up, or down in the simplest arcade style games, through to using sophisticated computer software to create a whole virtual world in which understanding and responding to the virtual inhabitants is a major key to success. Most games require a dogged determination to succeed despite myriad difficulties and multiple potential setbacks.

The increasing difficulty through levels of a computer game is resonant of working life, career progression or studying, with lessons learned in one sphere being useful in others. The element of novelty requires an ongoing openness and flexibility in perception – things are seldom just as they seem in the best games, with imagination and lateral thinking positively encouraged and rewarded.

At 3 my son was brilliant at Jigsaws and great at numbers but he wasn't interested in reading so much. When he then had his 'Game Boy' he was itching to play it and had to force himself to read the instructions so he could get onto the next levels... he then became an uber reader!

Having technology from a young age was great because he never craved it and would always allocate time accordingly. I noticed this more when in latter years some of his mates were being let loose on Xbox and they were seriously addicted, but because Paul has always had technology around him it's all been in his stride'.

Julie Bishop, mum to Paul (13)

Inventions

Games which require an element of inventiveness can be lots of fun. The creators of *Wallace and Gromit* teamed up with the UK Intellectual Property Office to promote the status of inventors and inventiveness to young people; they have some great games and resources on their website which encourage inventiveness and problem solving.

The site[43] contains a wealth of information, fun and games aimed at children from 4 to 16 years of age, including downloadable resources and online challenges such as *Sprocket Rocket* and *Invention Suspension*, as well as competitions to *Invent a Toy*, *Create a puppet show* and much more.

We're going on a Treasure Hunt

The possibilities for treasure hunts are endless, as is the fun for children of all ages, whether participating in an organised group or planning one at home. There are many different ways to run a treasure hunt, so here are just a few:

- *Themed* according to interest – e.g. Harry Potter, Myth and Magic, Nature, Space.
- *Community based* – pose questions about the local community which hunters have to research such as 'What type of ornament does No. 6 have in their front garden?', or 'Which community group uses the local hall on Thursdays at 6pm?'.

[43]http://www.wallaceandgromit.com/games/

- *Sensory/Identifying* – find items which represent the following: prickly, soft, rough, smooth and/or items which have points, are circular, triangular and so on.
- *Indoors* – these will probably need a little more thought, but use of cryptic clues can be quite amusing and non-literal, promoting imaginative thinking.

However your child completes a treasure hunt they are learning valuable social skills, experiencing how team work, persistence and focus can bring rewards.

WHAT YOUR CHILD IS LEARNING

Playing games provides a great opportunity to learn and develop many entrepreneurial characteristics, skills, and attitudes. Game playing is more than just wanting to win, it's about learning rules, how far they can be flexed, learning to work with others, and understanding and utilising what motivates opponents, recognising opportunities, then planning and working to realise them.

Games can hold up a mirror to life, with structure, rules, room for creativity, success or defeat. Games also provide a safe arena in which a child can experiment with their developing entrepreneurial skills – looking for opportunities, planning, resolutely persevering, dealing with failure or setback and learning from these to *keep on trying*.

Minding my own business

With so many leisure opportunities available to children, the idea that they might want to do what adults regard as work may seem counter-intuitive. However, if there is one thing that marks out the entrepreneur from the employee, it is precisely that child-like dissolution of the boundary between work and play that makes learning and creating fun, not drudgery.

As many of the interviews with young entrepreneurs show, children may well start to show an interest in business activities around this age. The young British inventor *Emily Cummins* spent much of her primary school years learning with the support of her granddad how to make toys from scrap materials, jewellery boxes, rabbit hutches and toy trucks as well as developing the skills to use the sander, pillar drill and the lathe. By the time *Jamie Dunn* was finishing primary school he already had plans for his first business: selling CDs to his teachers at school.

Whilst this book is about encouraging the development of entrepreneurial behaviour in its very broadest sense, if your child is showing genuine interest in, and passion for, doing something for themselves, and has responded positively to some of the activities, then this could be the time to introduce to them the concept of running a business. Try them out with a few of these activities to see how they get on, working out where their interests and skills lie.

ACTIVITIES

Lemonade stand

The idea of children setting up a lemonade stand over the summer has been around for a long time, yet it remains a popular activity, partly because it is relatively simple and inexpensive to set up, but also because it's such good fun on a hot, sunny afternoon. What your child will learn from setting up this kind of business will depend on just how involved they get in the process. The following areas all require discussion and planning, whatever kind of stand they decide to set up:

- *When?* Timing can be crucial – check if there's another event on locally, this could either work in your favour with lots of people around or work against you if it's a local fair and drinks are readily available there.
- *Where?* At this age you're probably looking at running the stand very locally, outside your own or at a friends' house with parental supervision. Just make sure they're somewhere that stock can be managed and replenished. Location is also important in determining how many people will pass by, unless they decide just to run it for invited friends only, in which case location is less of an issue.
- *How much?* Understanding how much potential customers will pay for the lemonade is important, so some basic research may be required (this could simply involve asking friends how much they would be prepared to pay, or checking out how much a bottle of lemonade costs in the local shop).
- *Marketing* – There are many different aspects to marketing a stand, from materials such as tablecloths through to promotional materials (a homemade banner?) and the price point. There's a good chance the cost of the lemonade is going to be much higher than those bought at a local shop, in which case talk with your child about ways to persuade people to part with their money. The stand may be raising funds for charity, in which case there is perhaps less sensitivity to price, but even so, ask them what they think is special about theirs, for example perhaps they have squeezed the lemons by hand.

So you can see, from a relatively simple concept such as running a lemonade stand, you and your child are discussing place, pricing, and promotion as well as learning to handle cash and customers.

Taking it online

The internet and the media upon it is the most valuable weapon you could arm your child with to connect globally, start up a business in Costa or get a job in China. What must happen is parents need to get up to speed with what's going on in our world and that technology is the new rock 'n' roll and if your child is not using it then you're allowing them to get left behind.

Julie Bishop, mum to Paul (13)

Depending on what interests your child, promoting their ideas could work well online. If, for example, they enjoy writing or poetry, drawing or photography, you may want to work with them to set up a website. If this is not something you've done before, it could be a great opportunity to learn with them.

Being in business, having a website and using social media go pretty much hand in hand these days, so giving your child the opportunity to learn the process of building a site and appropriate use of social media is a great skill developer. You'll need to take decisions about how extensively you want the site to be published, for example you could limit access by setting a password so that only known friends and family can access it initially. If, however, you are happy for it to be open access then make sure that basic parental controls are in place and be sure to monitor what your child is uploading and accessing and that they are not giving out personal information. A basic set of guidelines[44] has been developed by *Microsoft* covering children up to age 10 years, 11-14 and 15-18 years.

[44]http://www.microsoft.com/security/family-safety/childsafety-age.aspx

Much school Information Technology teaching is focused on helping children learn how to use particular programs (e.g. Excel, Word) and template driven web sites, as opposed to actually writing (programming) them. If your child shows an interest in how websites actually work, nurture that interest and get them involved from a programming perspective. There are a number of helpful online resources to nurture this interest and talent including *Codecademy*[45], a fun and interactive website for children (as well as adults) to visit and learn programming skills.

Learning to write code can be immensely satisfying and encourages a much more creative and enterprising way of engaging with technology than being simply a passive consumer or user of pre-programmed tools. There are numerous examples of software developers who became wealthy entrepreneurs, from Bill Gates to Mark Zuckerberg, not least because understanding how internet technology actually works, and being able to tinker 'under the bonnet' creates a tremendous opportunity for seeing what's possible. The mental discipline to doggedly pursue a dream despite setbacks and difficulties provides a context in which creativity and drive can result in real innovation and value.

Julie Bishop, mentioned earlier, explains how by the time her son Paul reached 13 he was competent in many of the skills needed to run an online business:

> *At 13 years old he now codes, creates web sites, is advanced at Photoshop, connects into talent communities on line where he thinks he might like to work and did a presentation in London the other day on what it's like to be an entrepreneur! He has asked if he can do his work experience at a company he's found in the U.S.A. His generation don't just look at what's available to them in their home town, they see the world as very small because they are connected*

[45]http://www.codecademy.com

with it continuously. He has overshot his teacher, my son learns everything he needs to know from Google and many others do too.

Making something out of (almost) nothing

If your child is at the higher end of this age range you may want to explore with them ways in which they can increase the amount of money they've have been given at birthday or Christmas times by setting up some kind of business or social enterprise as an alternative to the spend/save option.

Your child may have other ideas for running a business than a lemonade stand, which could be funded by just a small amount of money. Take a look at the video about 9 year old *Cain Monroy* who set up *Cain's Arcade*[46] during his summer holidays – not your normal run of the mill arcade but one made of disused cardboard! Building an arcade from cardboard boxes may not be what your child is interested in, but the more you can learn about what sparks their interest the easier it will be to help them find out whether running a business is for them.

> *Because we were running the business from home there were always lots of cars in the driveway so Ella and Paddy decided to earn some pocket money by washing the cars. They borrowed my bucket and sponge, put a notice up, and set to work. I remember they were delighted at how much they'd earned by the end of the day but I also recall their look of horror when I gave them my bill for the loan of the sponge and bucket!*
>
> **Paul Lindley, dad to Ella (12) and Paddy (9)**

Junior employee

There is a lot to be said for testing out a business idea on a part-time basis, particularly if you're considering giving up a full-time

[46]http://cainesarcade.com/

job. This 5-9 approach to starting a business is gaining in popularity and is a good way to test the market and see whether the idea 'has legs'.

If you are working at home or trying out a business idea then your child is likely to be curious about what you do (and sometimes a bit annoyed if you're working from home and answer the phone for business when you said you'd play with them!) so the more you can involve them in your work or business, the better chance there is they will understand what work is all about, and why you do it.

Take the opportunity to bring your child in to work with you to help out on the odd occasion; it's a great chance for them to see where you work and even help out if there are simple tasks such as putting letters in envelopes, packing up parcels, and general tidying up. If you're not able to take your child into your place of work, just think about the skills and attitudes you have and use during the course of your working day and find ways to model those to your child so that they can begin to learn them and build their own toolkit for the future.

WHAT YOUR CHILD IS LEARNING

In developing their own micro-business, no matter how sheltered the initial environment may be, the young entrepreneur must call upon those characteristics of imagination and inventiveness, ambition, resolve, and dealing with the emotional risks of failure (for this first business you'll probably not be re-mortgaging the house to provide capital so the risks are predominantly emotional not practical!). They must also learn to work with others and be focused on what they can do that is of value to others as well as themselves.

Interview with Paul Lindley, founder of *Ella's Kitchen*

PAUL LINDLEY is a multi-award winning entrepreneur and the founder of Ella's Kitchen – the organic food brand for babies and toddlers many parents (and little ones) will be familiar with, launched in 2006 and now turning over global retail sales of around £60million. Paul is dad to Ella (12) and Paddy (9).

Paul was born in Sheffield, but from the age of seven lived and grew up in Zambia with his parents, both civil servants. The difficulties of encouraging his fussy toddler daughter Ella to eat fruit and veg, and the realisation that he wasn't the only parent struggling with this, made Paul leave the security of what many considered to be the coolest job at Nickelodeon TV to develop and launch Ella's Kitchen.

TELL US ABOUT YOUR FAMILY BACKGROUND AND HOW YOUR PARENTS INFLUENCED YOUR DECISIONS ABOUT WORK.

'Although I came from a non-university family background, I was considered fairly smart and my parents encouraged me to follow the traditional route of going to university and securing a safe job, i.e. one for life. I felt they were always open to me finding new ways of doing things and would support me whatever I did.'

Paul completed his exams, including A levels, and went to study Pathology at university (his first attempt at doing something different). After a period of reflection, however, he decided he much preferred Economics and Politics so started his studies again. He went on to train and qualify as a chartered accountant which, of course, fitted well with his parents' encouragement of a more traditional career path. His subsequent move to children's TV channel, Nickelodeon, took him into a whole new world where a passion for putting children at the heart of everything they did whilst making it grown-up friendly made a real impact.

'My parents have always been very supportive of my career and work decisions,' says Paul, *'their strong values about the importance of education and hard work were always present.'* He goes on to explain that he was encouraged to question and keep an open mind to new ways of doing things – which is just as well given the decision he made in his mid-30s with two young children, to leave a good job (he was at the height of his career with Nickelodeon) and set up Ella's Kitchen. It was a decision that might well have caused some initial concern for his parents, but they remained supportive. Paul had both the experience and confidence to go it alone and had big ambitions from the start.

Interestingly, part-way through the interview Paul remembers that on his mother's side they were a family of builders. *'I'd completely forgotten that,'* he says, perhaps reflecting on whether some of that entrepreneurial drive had found itself in him from his mother's side of the family.

HOW DO YOU BELIEVE YOU ARE INFLUENCING YOUR OWN CHILDREN IN TERMS OF THEIR FUTURE WORK CHOICES, SKILLS, CHARACTERISTICS, AND IDEAS?

'They (Ella aged 12, Paddy aged 9) *are of course being brought up in a different generation, one in which they can do whatever they like,*

where there are no barriers to making their mark on the world,' says Paul, mentioning specifically the impact this has for girls.

He believes the pressure on children today is about believing things are easy (citing *The X Factor*) and children in this age range (4-14) *'are fearless of being wrong'.*

'There are three important elements of being an entrepreneur,' says Paul, and goes on to name these as Creativity, Passion, and Tenacity. In children, including his own, he believes that creativity is easily encouraged and can be taught through everyday parenting, not just painting or model-making, but through their play in general and how they learn to channel creativity and develop their view of the world. *'Passion is about exploring with your child what really gets to them in terms of interest. Tenacity, well that's about going the extra mile, to be persistent and think about how things can be better next time around. Ella and I say, "What do quitters do? They quit." It's important to encourage them to go the extra mile to do the extra thing which will achieve results.'*

Paul notices all three elements in his children and believes you can spot them quite easily. *'If you have more than one child, it's also easy to notice the differences between them, and it's not always the academically bright ones who shine through,'* he comments.

He is also clear what he wants for his own children: *'I want them to do something because of a passion rather than because of money.'* His children have a broad awareness of the basics of business and increasingly he takes his children to work. Indeed, he encourages many of his employees to do the same during the school holidays.

'In fact,' he says, *'there are a group of six year olds visiting the company at the moment who are telling us all about what they think organic means, what friendship means, and what they would change in the world. They are unencumbered with the issues adults have,'* says Paul, *'and it is both remarkable and humbling.'* The video

recording of what the six year olds had to say can be viewed online.[47]

AS AN EMPLOYER WITH OVER 40 STAFF, WHAT DO YOU LOOK FOR IN YOUR NEW RECRUITS?

'It's about a mindset,' he replies. *'We're looking for an overlap of values between ours and theirs as that's crucial to our brand. We have, for example, rejected people with a better skillset simply because there was no alignment of values. Yes, we have a threshold of skills that have to be met, but beyond that it's very much about their mindset and how they have lived their values.'*

Paul goes on to talk about the culture of the company, using words such as 'open', 'motivating' and 'entrepreneurial', although he stresses that he's not looking specifically for any more entrepreneurs to join the team. *'We don't want everyone being entrepreneurial,'* he says. He recently gave everyone a day off from the office to do whatever they wanted, telling them *'Do some research, go for a walk, whatever you want,'* to come up with ideas about how to fulfil the company's long-term goals and ambitions. This approach to taking the business forward arguably requires staff to possess or develop all three entrepreneurial elements Paul identified earlier – Creativity, Passion, and Tenacity.

CAN YOU GIVE PARENTS YOUR TOP TIPS?

'Be realistic with your children,' says Paul, recalling his earlier comment about the pressure on children to believe things are easy these days. *'Take time to teach them underlying values and never let them accept mediocrity. Look for and help your child develop sets of skills, notice how they play, recognise and support their developing skills and characteristics of Creativity, Passion, and Tenacity.'*

[47]http://www.ellaskitchen.co.uk/the-good-stuff-we-do/

'*Explore with your child what interests them,*' he continues, '*and encourage them to keep trying and building on what they are learning.*'

On a final note, Paul recalls one of Ella and Paddy's first ventures into entrepreneurial activities when they were aged just seven and four '*Because we were running the business from home there were always lots of cars in the driveway so Ella and Paddy decided to earn some pocket money by washing the cars. They borrowed my bucket and sponge, put a notice up, and set to work. I remember they were delighted at how much they'd earned by the end of the day, but I also recall their look of horror when I gave them my bill for the loan of the sponge and bucket!*' Guess that's the 'be realistic' part of Paul's parenting coming out!

Team challenge, team fun

Managing risk, room for growth

Curious kids

Stretch and challenge

A future vision

Get crafty and creative

The business of money

Ambition and aspirations – you can get it (if you *really* want)

Team challenge, team fun

An entrepreneur is a creator of value and for anything of value to be realised, an element of collaboration, in business as in life, is necessary. No one works in a vacuum; we all require the support and cooperation of others to achieve our goals in life. Collaboration involves a willingness to listen and to learn as well as being able to communicate our ideas to others.

Because we can achieve more when we all work together using our different skills, the whole being greater than the sum of its parts, the enterprising child will learn to recognise the talents of others and motivate them to contribute to a joint project, and will need to be able to work as part of a team where required.

Whether you have a small or a large family, home provides a perfect setting for teaching your child about teamwork, leadership, delegation and cooperation, and the activities below are suggested as ways of helping your child explore what it means to be part of a team in a supportive setting.

ACTIVITIES
Top dog

Very few children relish the idea of doing chores around the home. With some creativity, though, you can make them fun. At this age your child can take on more responsibility for chores; to help them learn the true value of teamwork, resist the urge to dictate which chores they should do, instead, discuss and plan chores together.

A fun game is 'top dog' where your child gets to be the boss. The boss gets to decide which chores need to be carried out, what equipment is required for each task and who carries out particular chores. Allow your child free reign – this needs to be fun – but don't offer any guidance other than a pen and paper.

The first thing your child learns from this activity is that efficient teamwork usually requires someone to be in charge, a concept they will already be familiar with from school life with its teachers, sports team captains and so on.

How are teams managed so as to get the best out of each team member and so that the task can be completed effectively? The chances are that your child will have relished their new-found role as boss and simply delegated each task with glee. If there are siblings, there might be a squabble as to who does each job – highly likely in fact! How will they resolve this? Will they strike a bargain or use some crafty negotiation techniques? Are the tasks allocated appropriately so that they are achievable by, for example, younger siblings or less able members of the family? Are they showing consideration to others?

Discuss afterwards who gets to be top dog next time round, and what lessons have been learned. The idea is not to berate anyone or to make comparisons, but simply to explore the way in which everyone has a role to play in working as a team, and that 'leadership' itself is more a matter of collaboration than hierarchy. Whatever authority and sanctions they might wield, a leader without willing followers will never achieve as much as one who can bring out the best in their team members. This is a straightforward activity providing opportunities to learn how to pull together as a team, to communicate effectively and how to develop simple negotiation techniques. As in all attempts at collaboration, there are possibilities for conflict, but that makes it valuable, because learning to deal with emotional conflicts and to facilitate altruistic cooperation over natural egocentricity is the essence of effective team building. For the entrepreneurial individual who has clear ideas of what they want to achieve, but requires the cooperation of others to achieve their goals, learning to work with others effectively may be a life-long learning process, so your child needs all the support you can give them at this stage.

'What do you think?'

From time to time there will be situations in the family which call for much larger decisions to be taken, for example, the purchase of a new car or moving into a new home.

Involving your child in this decision making process will allow them to express their opinion and potentially influence the outcome. If you are thinking of moving to a new home, let them help decide how it will be decorated – or at the very least their own bedroom, even if the decision to move itself is non-negotiable.

If you are buying a new car, you could discuss your budget and ask them what type of car they think you should buy. While their choice of car might be totally unsuitable, you are at least teaching them valuable communication skills – talking, listening and negotiating. You are also modeling the important principle that the team leader who involves their team members in the decision making process and seeks to give them a voice, will build a more harmonious team in which everyone feels valued, and will gain better team 'buy-in' for important decisions.

This habit of discussing purchasing decisions doesn't have to be confined to major ones like houses or cars; getting children into the habit of listening to and expressing reasons for purchasing decisions is a great way to develop their thinking and communication skills, preparing them for active and effective participation in teams in the future. There is scope to relate even simple purchasing decisions as the brand of juice you buy to wider economic and ethical questions, such as which brands are 'best value', which are awful but rely upon having a household label, which companies are involved in unethical practices, or should your tea be Fair Trade, organic.

Geocache hide and seek

This modern variation of traditional hide and seek is fun, active and teaches your child valuable team playing skills at the same time. Geocaching is a real outdoor treasure hunt game where players try to locate hidden containers (called caches) at various locations, using GPS-enabled devices.

Simply register at the web site[48], enter your post code for the nearest cache then download the co-ordinates to your smartphone or GPS enabled device. Depending on where the cache is located, you can play this game on foot, by car or on bicycles.

This game involves you all working together as a team – reading (indeed deciphering) the map co-ordinates and translating them into appropriate routes, finding each clue, inevitably getting lost and trying to find the correct route again. It is great fun and teaches the valuable lesson that effective communication between team members is vital for success. Your child is also learning that everyone has strengths and weaknesses, but the success of a team is dependent upon everyone playing to their strengths.

Whistle while you work

If there are occasions when you work from home, find opportunities for your child to carry out or help you with tasks, if not during the course of a normal working week, then during half-term and holidays.

Discuss your typical work day and the tasks you need to complete. Have fun together and think about how you can swap roles, allowing your child to be team leader. Some employers participate in 'Take your Son/Daughter to Work' initiatives. This is a fun yet practical way of showing your child what you do at work.

[48]www.geocaching.com

Be prepared... be very prepared

To give your child opportunities for engaging in fun and effective team based tasks, you could consider suggesting they enroll in their local Cub Scouts[49] or Brownies[50] group (UK Scouts enroll at age 10½ and UK Girl Guides at age 10); there they are likely to get involved in just the kind of team based, indoor and outdoor pursuits that companies pay large sums of money to send their executives on, precisely because of their value in building the capacity for team working and leadership.

WHAT YOUR CHILD IS LEARNING

Few entrepreneurs succeed by working entirely alone. They are adept at collaborating with others to share their goal. Without exception, all employers would prefer someone who is a good team player, with a willingness to adapt, be flexible and co-operative.

The activities and ideas above are designed to develop your child's capacity to work within or lead a team and will help develop valuable communication skills, including how to negotiate and motivate. Accomplishing tasks together reinforces teamwork, the value of working together towards one common goal. The family is the first team your child is a member of, and what they learn in the home team will shape their attitudes and character for years to come.

[49]http://scouts.org.uk – UK Cubs and Scouts are for boys or girls
[50]http://www.girlguiding.org.uk – UK Brownies and Girl Guides are for girls only

Managing risk, room for growth

Entrepreneurs are prepared to take controlled risks in the pursuit of value and must be comfortable with taking responsibility for their own decisions and their outcome. As children grow up, they need increasing independence to make their own decisions and they must learn to manage risk and take responsibility for their acts and omissions.

One of the most important aspects of being able to make decisions is self-confidence. If a person is confident in their ability to analyse a situation, they will feel confident enough to make the right decision.

As a parent, you can help your child develop confidence, experience and judgment by being prepared to let go and allow them to make age-appropriate decisions. Your child needs confidence in their own ability to act appropriately, as well as in line with their personal values.

Whatever your goal is, believe you can do it and don't be afraid to fail. I don't care if I fail, obviously I never aim to fail and I always aim to win in everything I do, but if I do fail then I take all the positives I can from it, although I'm still annoyed!

James Headspeath, student and young entrepreneur

ACTIVITIES

'Mum/Dad, I forgot my...'

As parents, we know that children learn by their mistakes, yet we still insist on running around after them 'just in case they forget'.

You're not a bad parent if you 'allow' your child to forget to do or pack something, once in a while. Forgetting is part of life, but you can help your child to develop appropriate habits of mind that will enable them minimise their own mistakes themselves and, where they do fail to remember something, to help them understand that they need to take responsibility for their actions and deal with the consequences.

Think of all the things that you might currently remember to do for your child, for example:

- Iron their school clothes
- Put out their school clothes for the next day
- Pack their reading journal/homework
- Put their packed lunch where they will see it before they leave for school
- Put dirty washing in the laundry basket

And probably far more besides!

Look at your own list and ask what you can trust your child to do for themselves. If the answer is 'not a lot', then it may be you are excessively fearful of the consequences of them forgetting. Ask yourself what is the worst that could happen and whether or not it might actually contribute more to their growth to allow them to 'fail' than to over-protect them.

For example, what is the worst that could happen if they forget to pack their P.E. kit? If the school has a policy of 'no kit, no P.E.' you can probably bet they won't forget again – unless they absolutely hate P.E.

You may not feel comfortable allowing your nine-year-old to do their own ironing, but can they at least put aside their school clothes for the next day? What are the consequences of them getting this wrong, or just failing to do it: minutes lost the next morning while they try to find something to wear? If the knock on effect of this is that they are late for school, which in turn results in a 'Late Slip', or some other form of penalty, aren't they less likely to forget again?

An important aspect of making good decisions is looking back on past ones in order to learn from them. In fact, your child needs to make mistakes and bad decisions to enable that learning to take place, so taking all responsibility away from them may well hinder their growth in confidence, good judgment and independence.

Managing risk
For your child to begin to make their own well-informed decisions they will need to learn to assess and manage a degree of risk. This is a difficult area for parents, but it is true that, whilst we obviously have a duty to protect our children from serious risks, it is also easy to be over-protective. No child ever learned to ride a bike without falling off many times in their first years of riding and, similarly, any worthwhile achievement carries the attendant risk of failure or at the very least setbacks and scrapes along the way.

Risk is often considered in the narrow context of the physical – falling over when learning to walk or run, falling out of trees and so on, but in a broad sense risk is involved in any situation where something new and unfamiliar is being attempted. The 'slings and arrows' that await us can be emotional or social as well as physical, as any shy teenager experiences when venturing to ask for a date or joining a new class. One of the risks that can inhibit creativity and learning in children of this age is 'failure' and it is important for children to learn that failure is not to be feared, but rather welcomed as an opportunity to learn and improve performance.

Given that risk is inevitable, your child needs a number of things from you. The first is information, since without relevant and accurate information risk cannot be assessed. So if they are going to climb that tree then a lesson in tree climbing, and some discussion of the things to watch out for (e.g. rotting branches) could be useful; if they are going to use the internet for learning, skills development and entertainment then some age appropriate knowledge of possible risks associated with for example social networking, but more importantly knowledge of how to minimise risk (such as not publishing personal information, their address or telephone number), would be a very good idea[51].

Information also comes from experience, so by allowing your child to take responsibility for issues such as remembering to take their P.E. kit to school, you are helping them to build up experience, whereas if they are protected from the consequences of forgetting (in this example), they also lose the opportunity to gain experience of those consequences and add that to their store of knowledge.

The second and third things your child needs to deal with risk are courage and vision – characteristics that have already been discussed, and here it is only really necessary to say that encouraging them to visualise the desired goal is a great way to motivate your child to face and overcome their fear.

The final thing your child needs is the ability to assess analytically the nature and degree of any risk. Analysis of risk makes the difference between calculated and proportional risk-taking, where the benefits outweigh the risks and the riskiest elements can be identified, minimised or removed in some way, and recklessness.

Analysis of risk is also a good way of developing the mental discipline of controlling or putting aside emotional reactions such as fear, where appropriate, in order to achieve a desired goal. This is what climbers do all the time; they know that fear and panic are more likely to result in a fall than disciplined focus.

You can help your child get used to dealing with risk without exposing them to disproportionate danger by enrolling them in clubs or organisations that provide access to 'adventure' activities under safe supervision. Children will naturally seek out excitement and challenge, so providing access to these things in an environment where they will also learn about the dangers and

[51]http://www.microsoft.com/en-gb/security/family-safety/childsafety-age.aspx

safety precautions (of heights, rivers, the sea, the great outdoors, skateboarding and so on) will provide them with a far safer and more satisfying outlet than they will find, for example, climbing over garage roofs or playing 'chicken' with the traffic.

We cannot shield our children from risk. They will need to learn the consequences of misjudging risk – as painful as that might be for them and us as parents, but enabling them to experience these in a managed way will prepare them for taking calculated risks in later life.

WHAT YOUR CHILD IS LEARNING

An entrepreneur must be comfortable with the idea of risk, for in the creation of anything worthwhile the old adage "nothing ventured, nothing gained" certainly applies. On the other hand an entrepreneur must be able to assess degrees of risk and come to an informed decision about the relative benefits and risks that any course of action presents. For this they need knowledge, confidence in their own judgment and the prudence to know when it may be worth seeking a second opinion. They also need the ability to formulate a plan to minimise risk exposure and create back–up plans in the event that something they identify as a risk does actually occur.

The aim of the activities in this section is to encourage your child to become confident in making well informed decisions, to be someone not content to simply follow the crowd or reliant upon others to tell them what to do. By providing opportunities for your child to identify and manage risk, and take responsibility for their own actions you are helping your child to grow in confidence, wisdom, and the courage to create.

Curious kids

We lead such busy lives and can be so focused on getting from A to B that we forget to enjoy the ride along the way. There is also an on-going debate as to whether, with so many different methods of assessing school based performance, children's formal education stifles creativity and curiosity.

Certainly by the time children reach this age range, most mainstream schools will have already moved away from encouraging learning through play to a more academic approach to study.

There is still, though, ample opportunity for home based activities with an emphasis on learning through having fun, to continue harnessing the creativity inherent in a child's sense of wonder and natural curiosity.

Curiosity is an essential trait of the entrepreneurial mindset; it leads to exploration, to discovery, to envisioning new possibilities and focusing on realising them. Children need space to discover the world around them and to enjoy learning, to experiment, and to learn through failure as much as through success rather than risk having their creativity stifled by an overbearing need to 'get it right' or fulfill educational targets. As parents you can give your children these opportunities in a way that is difficult for schools burdened with large class sizes and the pressure to achieve set targets and a good league table ranking.

Encourage your child to be inquisitive about the things they experience in their everyday life and you will help to set a pattern of engagement with the world that will enhance their enjoyment of life and ability to engage with its challenges in an enthusiastic and productive way – the hallmark of the enterprising child.

Exploration

An excellent science program on ABC TV called *'Backyard Science'*[52] teaches science by showing children how to conduct experiments in their backyard. All the experiments are simple, fun and use materials within and around the home. For example:

- *What happens when you place a Softmint™ in a bottle of fizzy pop?* Do make sure this experiment is tried in the backyard!
- *Can you cook food without a cooker?*
- *How do you make perfume?*

If you have access to it, encourage your child to watch this programme with you. Alternatively, the internet has many websites with similar backyard science activities. The Science Museum[53] has fun activities which can be played online as well as a free download of 'Kitchen Science' – experiments for the home using utensils and ingredients easily available in the kitchen.

Debate

There are, of course, different ways for your child to explore – with thought as well as with body, indeed philosophers and scientists have developed the concept of the *Gedankenexperiment*[54] ('thought experiment') to describe one aspect of this process.

Debating is a very good way to explore different ideas, viewpoints and opinions, and mediate between them. These skills will help your child learn to articulate the reasons for their viewpoint; true debating is not about resorting to rhetoric, not about asserting your views as forcefully as possible.'

[52]http://www.abc.net.au/abc3/shows/3949.htm
[53]The Science Museum 'Kitchen Science' http://www.sciencemuseum.org.uk/educators/classroom_and_homework_resources/resources/
[54]http://en.wikipedia.org/wiki/Thought_experiment

There are plenty of opportunities to open age-appropriate debates with your child on social issues. The main thing is to find something that engages them emotionally, and then to help them learn the vital skill of being able to understand – still better to argue against – competing points of view. When it comes to environmental issues or animal welfare (fox hunting, meat eating, the fur trade etc.), you may find yourself playing devil's advocate, encouraging your child to argue back to objections to their position. The object of the exercise is not for you as an adult to 'win' the argument, but to encourage your child to understand the 'rules of the debating game', to relish exploring the logical issues, and to gain a respect for rational analysis and for people who hold a different point of view to theirs. Having these discussions helps your child to recognise and explore what they like and dislike, what is fair and unfair, or what is right and wrong. By sharing and learning to justify their opinion on these simple issues (and at this point we are talking about simple, age appropriate topics that you as a parent are happy to raise with them) they begin to have a sense of what matters to them.

Your child's developing ability to reflect upon and justify their values has major importance in developing entrepreneurial characteristics; entrepreneurs need to have a sense of the solidity of their position, and to have critically examined and tested in the fire of reason and doubt their most cherished projects if they are to have the tenacity to persevere in the face of setbacks and skepticism from others.

WHAT YOUR CHILD IS LEARNING

This section began by reflecting upon the importance of curiosity and moved through the role of physical experimentation and enquiry into the development of intellectual curiosity and the role of reasoned debate in exploring the world of value. This stuff is central to the development of entrepreneurial characteristics. The entrepreneur is by nature inquisitive, but also possesses the ability to focus their energy based on a rational evaluation of what is possible and what needs to be overcome.

Once the entrepreneurial person has a goal in mind they will investigate all the possible options and determine the best way to eliminate any obstacles to that goal. The activities in this section embrace both science and philosophy, and are designed to help your child develop an inquiring mind and critical thinking skills in making sense of their discoveries and observations. The activities are also useful ways of finding out what their passion is, what interests them and makes them want to find out more, and in developing a sense of self-reliance.

Stretch and challenge

I like the idea of not being part of the crowd. I hate the humdrum of being 'normal'. I love to be able to continually push myself. So that would be my other piece of advice – stretch yourself.

Timothy Armoo, young entrepreneur and founder of EntrepreneurXpress

Entrepreneurs frequently require the ability to 'go it alone' and think for themselves, indeed there may be times when the only advice received from others is to 'give up', so they need to develop self-reliance and confidence in their ability to think their way through problems.

When a child has an issue or problem, the natural tendency as a parent is to rush in and tell them how to fix it. While there are times when this approach is entirely appropriate, it is generally a good thing to encourage children to think for themselves, to develop analytical thinking, the ability to be able to break down and look at a problem in different ways and come up with solutions.

When you stretch and challenge your child's mind, you are encouraging them to think in a different way, to evaluate all the available information and determine whether a decision is right from either a practical or an ethical point of view.

Analytical thinking requires an open-mind to consider alternative ways of looking at situations. This is likely to help your child develop greater empathy for others as they understand the reasoning and assumptions behind individual and group decision making. The ability to critically engage with others' viewpoints is also a valuable counterweight to our natural tendency to tribalism. In the long run your child will be better able to arrive at their own political and philosophical perspectives, be able to justify their position and less likely to be negative towards those who disagree with them. As your child becomes a young teenager, they will need these critical thinking skills to be able to make decisions independently of you. It is perfectly ok to not know the answer – this is about them learning what to do when they don't know.

The following activities help your child develop the skills necessary to listen, analyse and interpret information in order to make a decision.

ACTIVITIES

Making connections

Puzzles and problem solving games – from classic examples such as chess to computer games and apps designed to stimulate logical thought – are excellent ways to help your child to develop critical, logical and problem solving skills. These types of games reinforce logic, visualisation and creative thinking. Through them your child is learning how to make connections, to experiment, visualise and work consequences through in their heads. 'What happens if I do this, what will follow from it and what will be the consequences of that happening? Suppose I do that instead?'

Analytical skills are useful for your child so they are able to break down a problem into its elements, analyse it, identify the variables (what can be changed in any given situation/decision) and test in their mind the possible or inevitable consequences of each variation in each variable in order to move forward.

Taking it outside

Sometimes it can help to externalise this analytical process as we do not all have the capacity of chess Grand Masters to hold vast numbers of patterns and consequences in our heads. Making notes on paper, drawing rough and ready diagrams, mind-mapping or writing about a problem, for example in a diary, all helps to externalise the process of thinking things through and unpack the problem.

The surest way to help someone to externalise and think through a problem is good old fashioned human conversation – the essence of much human problem solving.

When your child is presented with a problem or decision you can help by encouraging them to break down the problem into bite sized pieces and identify those elements that can and cannot be changed. With some problems there may appear to be nothing that can be changed, but the way we think about the situation cannot be taken away from us, so we always have the choice to change ourselves.

You can help your child by using open-ended questions and prompting. For example, to a common issue:

"I don't know where to start with my homework."

You might ask questions such as:

- *'Is this to do with this particular piece of homework, or is it about wanting to do something else instead?'*
- *'What can you change and what is non-negotiable here?'*
- *'Are there any parts of your homework that you are confident about tackling?'*
- *'Are there parts that you have a particular problem with?'*
- *'What do you need to know to be able to tackle the parts you're having a problem with?'*

Prompting your child in these ways encourages them to identify, categorise, analyse and find solutions to problems. It is also something you can consciously model yourself when faced with problems. Why not make it a two-way street and talk to your children about appropriate issues that you need to decide on too, so that you can start to tackle them together?

Think about thinking

When faced with questions, children often try to second guess adults, providing an answer that they think we want to hear rather than what they really think or want to say. It is also possible for children to internalise parental opinions so that they suppress what they truly think or feel themselves and adapt to parental beliefs and systems of reasoning, which in themselves may not always be wholly rational. It is therefore good to get the message across that independent and successful analytical thinking starts with being honest with themselves as well as with others. In this way children can be encouraged to start properly thinking about their own thinking (this is known as *metacognition*[55]) and can adopt a reflectively critical attitude to their own reasoning which is the foundation of effective analytical thinking and problem solving.

By providing an environment where your child feels safe from ridicule, you can encourage thinking about thinking by simply asking your child's opinion of things they read about, items in the news or what is happening in their life and immediate environment such as school, church, clubs etc. Include discussion and debate among the family within a relaxed atmosphere to understand and learn to respect differing views. Resist the temptation to win the argument or ensure that your child's opinions mirror your own; the aim is to encourage your child *how* to think, not *what* to think.

Once you have decided upon a topic that your child has raised or you know they are familiar with, the most important questions are effective starter questions:

- *What do you think about...?*
- *What would you do about...?*

---

[55]http://dictionary.reference.com/browse/metacognition

Good questions to get your child thinking about thinking are:

- *What would happen if...?*
- *Does that mean that you think...?*
- *How would that work?*
- *What do you think we can learn from that?*
- *What's the moral of the story?*
- *What do you think they believe about...?*

Your child is at an age where they can start to think logically and reason abstractly, but there will still be a tendency towards concrete thinking and not being able to see beyond actualities, so don't expect too much of them. On the other hand do not expect too little – being able to deal in abstractions and categories such as causality, presuppositions and consequences is part of our birthright as humans and even children as young as six[56] have been shown to be capable of thinking philosophically – the essence of meta-cognition and analytical thinking.

Other ways to help your child think analytically is to encourage them to ask for an explanation or clarification if they don't understand something. It's perfectly ok not to know the answer to all questions, in fact it's a given and therefore essential to adopt certain strategies to find the answer to questions, including seeking clarification of what you do and do not know or understand.

Encourage your child to research solutions for themselves. Using a simple example, a very common problem is the question, *'How do I spell...?';* instead of spelling the word for them, encourage them to use a dictionary. Scientific and technical questions may stump you, but the internet is bound to have accessible answers somewhere and by using the internet you are both modeling that essential self-honesty about what you do and do not know (never

[56]http://www.guardian.co.uk/education/2007/dec/04/highereducation.news

be tempted to bluff even if you think you *should* know), and the usefulness of self-directed research.

WHAT YOUR CHILD IS LEARNING

Entrepreneurs rarely have all the answers, but through a process of analytical thinking and problem solving techniques they know what to do in order to find an answer. Knowing what you don't know and finding ways to work out what you need to know, including drawing on the knowledge and expertise of others where appropriate, is the mark of true wisdom.

In these activities your child is being encouraged to pursue intellectual honesty and analytical rigor as positive ends in themselves, and also as a means to developing a secure foundation for their knowledge and decision making. This is an absolutely essential component of the entrepreneurial approach to life, for without this rigour and honesty the entrepreneurial capacity to envision better futures would be only so much wishful thinking, and their tenacity in the face of opposition simply blind stubbornness.

Stretching and challenging your child to think for themselves builds their confidence to move forward and take calculated risks based on careful consideration of all the factors involved; these are skills they will need for the rest of their life.

A future vision

The entrepreneurial journey, whilst needing many practical skills, is guided by a sense of vision, the ability to imagine and be motivated by what is not yet real, by the power of an idea. Entrepreneurs are visionaries, so to nurture your child's visionary capacity it is necessary to expand their horizons beyond the everyday.

In this section we consider three ways of encouraging this capacity to look beyond the obvious: the first a simple raising of the eyes upwards – inspiration to artists and visionaries throughout the centuries; the second suggests the enriching effect that exposure to unfamiliar cultures and ideas can have; and finally a fun activity for promoting the imaginative use of what is given, in the art of storytelling.

ACTIVITIES

The sky at night
Children are frequently fascinated with space, from science fiction themes of time travel including contemporary mythology of that well known travelling Time Lord, the grand space opera of *Star Wars*, space rockets, aliens and astronauts, or simply the vast starry night and the hope of one day seeing a comet arc across the night sky.

Nurture in your child a fascination for the universe and for our planet Earth: the way it moves, our proximity to the other planets, the constellations and much more. Step outside and look up at the sky at night: even urban skies can provide a beautiful show on a clear night.

Borrow books from the library to learn about the different constellations together. Can your child identify the North Star? What are the names of the constellations? The well-known ones are the Plough, the Big Dipper and Orion. What are the others and where did the names come from? The *Star Walk* app[57] is a great resource which labels all the stars, constellations, and satellites an iPhone is pointed at as well as providing facts and graphics.

How many planets are there in our solar system? (The official answer is no longer nine.) What are their names in correct order from the Sun? What are the distances of the planets from the Sun? How long might it take to reach one of them by rocket? Is Saturn the only planet with rings and what are these rings made of?

What link is there between the moon and the tides of the oceans?

Help your child to investigate these fascinating facts and so many more. Older children can be encouraged to research these facts by themselves with books borrowed from the library or through research on the internet. If they show an interest in taking the subject further, consider enrolling them into astronomy clubs, many of which are free to join.

It may be that your child takes an interest in cosmology, in which case you can have lots of fun exploring some of the strange answers to perennial childhood questions that science has offered. You can encourage your child in their questioning, as they wonder whether you can ever reach the edge of the universe, what happened before the big bang, whether we all are literally made of stardust, and that's before you get round to exploring the mystery of time and space, the expanding universe, worm holes and black holes.

It doesn't matter that at this age very few children will be able to understand the further reaches of cosmological theory or the second law of thermo-dynamics; many ideas will be familiar to them from science fiction and there is a good chance that you won't know much more than they do unless you happen to be a scientist yourself. What matters is that you are willing to undertake the journey with them, to ask the questions and encourage them to explore possible answers, to get the feeling that there are mysteries to be solved and

[57]http://itunes.apple.com/gb/app/star-walk-5-stars-astronomy/id295430577?mt=8

questions which have multiple answers because there are things about the universe that we just don't really know yet.

It is hard not to think about the vastness of the universe without gaining a new sense of perspective on everyday priorities. Underlying all the scientific questions there is, of course, an ancient and perennial sense of wonder at the fact of existence and inevitable speculation as to its purpose and point.

So we recommend star-gazing; it's a great way to encourage your child not to take the world and conventional wisdom for granted, to develop a questioning and probing mind and a real sense of new possibilities and perspectives waiting to be discovered.

Cultural connections

Each and every family has its own micro-culture, its set of rules and assumptions, shared beliefs and values and is part of a wider culture. As parents we naturally want to pass on the riches of our particular cultural tradition. Whilst this is understandable it is also worth considering whether there are elements in other cultures that can be looked to for good ideas and practices that may help to develop your child's entrepreneurial characteristics.

One of the benefits of living in a multi-cultural society is that we can look beyond our own culture for ideas and inspiration and we can also encourage our children to explore alternative ways of seeing the world, which can be especially effective in helping them to develop a sense of possibility and the ability to think innovatively and outside the box.

An interesting example of the impact of multi-cultural experiences is to be found in the life and work of David Adjaye OBE who was born in Dar es Salaam Tanzania, to Ghanaian parents. Very early on in his life, he experienced cultures from several different communities - Christian, Indian, Muslim and Sikh - having lived in Tanzania, Egypt, Yemen, Lebanon and finally Britain.

In an interview with CNN's *African Voices*[58], he revealed that he originally had not thought of becoming an architect. However, after exploring a foundation in the arts, he realised that his entire background had shaped his appreciation of space' in relation to the way different communities live:

David Adjaye © Ed Reeve

I don't know whether my father engineered this, but very early on I came into contact with different cultures and different ways of living. It was through this pot-pourri of experiences, of living in West Africa, North Africa, and the Middle East and mixing with all these groups, which allowed me to sample many different spatial and cultural conditions. Later, by the time I was 19 years old, I realised that this had a profound effect on my relationship with people. I became very sensitive about that.

Adjaye was awarded the OBE for services to architecture in 2007 and his global practice has won a number of prestigious commissions, the biggest and most recent being for the Moscow School of Management.

While you may not be able to travel extensively with your child, you can make a simple trip to your local museum or art gallery, many of which are free. In larger cities, there are often cultural events or festivals; take whatever opportunities there are to expose your child to different cultural traditions and ways of seeing.

Can you share your own cultural experiences, that of your family, ancestors, or even of close friends? Download and explore Google Earth. Make a point of planning your virtual vacation ahead of time, so that your child knows where you will be 'visiting' next. You can

[58]Source: CNN African Voices: 'David Adjaye's journey into art', interview with David Adjaye November 2011.

then encourage them to carry out research projects on different countries and cultures.

These activities are not intended to bring about a sort of hazy cultural relativism, the idea that all cultural practices or beliefs are equal with no way of adjudicating between them (which is the criticism occasionally leveled at multiculturalism) on the contrary, they are about being freed from unreflective acceptance of cultural traditions. The aim is to develop methods of critical thinking about cultural, political, and ethical issues whilst freeing the imagination to consider possible new ways of doing things.

Creating a story from random elements

Entrepreneurs are adept at taking the disparate elements of everyday life and weaving them into a new narrative resulting in the creation of value; they see patterns and possibilities where others may just see random juxtaposition.

In the following activity you and your child can experience the imaginative ordering of elements to create something of value, whilst having a lot of fun in the process.

Take a sheet of paper and write on it random nouns (you can make a game of how you decide on this list as a later elaboration), then find a hat or bag, and a standard kitchen timer, or other timing device (e.g. stopwatch or mobile phone).

The nouns are separated into individual slips of paper, folded and placed in the hat/bag. The first player draws from the hat/ bag three slips of paper and looks at them; the others draw three slips but must place them in front of them unfolded. The first player starts a story (a time limit should be imposed, we recommend three minutes) which incorporates in some way their three items (e.g. a cabbage, a computer, an elephant), keeping going until the timer signals the end of the allocated time.

The next player turns over their three nouns from the hat/bag and must continue with the story incorporating their three elements, and so on. The game can finish after an agreed number of turns, time, or when you have run out of nouns in the hat.

For extra fun you could record the story telling. You could also experiment with varying the number of nouns (e.g. increase by one every turn, so it can get hilarious/ingenious as a player eventually struggles to incorporate 10 random elements into three minutes of story) and introducing adjectives and verbs. There are plenty of ways to make this activity great fun for your particular family situation.

WHAT YOUR CHILD IS LEARNING

One of the most essential elements of the entrepreneurial character is the ability to look at the world and see patterns and possibilities; to bring together ideas from different areas in a creative fusion. This is especially true of inventors, but any entrepreneur who sees an unfulfilled need and a way to provide for that need is exhibiting the same ability to create something new from what is given, to perceive possibilities where others only see facts.

The activities in this section are designed to help develop and nurture this all important trait by:

- Freeing perception and imagination from conventional or traditional thinking to allow imagination to flourish
- Encouraging a sense of wonder and possibility
- Encouraging the perception of patterns and connections
- Promoting critical thinking and analysis
- Encouraging imagination and creativity

Get crafty and creative

Entrepreneurs have an ability to create something from scratch, to perceive possibilities that others have not yet seen or have overlooked. An enterprising mind is an innovative, creative mind.

Very young children are naturally curious. For example, they may often ask, 'What's that?' or spend a seemingly endless amount of time exploring a cardboard box, but to help our children develop their creativity into their teens and beyond we should continue providing stimulating projects or surroundings which fuel their curiosity and encourage their creativity.

> *My parents were quite frugal and pocket money was kept to a minimum. Finding ways to supplement the cash was a constant source of entertainment. My brothers and I would try anything to earn a little holiday money, from picking fruit, to selling strawberries on the main road or making cakes to sell to neighbours.*
>
> **Laura Tenison MBE, founder and CEO of JoJo Maman Bébé**

ACTIVITIES

Creative projects around the home

Encourage your child to create craft projects around the home. This needn't be an expensive exercise. There are a number of websites which show how to create projects for free, or by using materials that would normally be thrown away.

However, while making these crafts projects are fun in themselves, you can develop your child's curiosity and creativity even further by encouraging them to change or improve upon the initial design. So, for example, balsa – a lightweight and inexpensive wood – can be easily crafted to make simple models such as sailing boats, gliders, etc. At first, encourage your child to closely follow the instructions so that the model is made exactly as is. After they have become comfortable, or maybe even bored with their first design, encourage them to improve upon it.

How can you make this boat faster? Will you need to change its shape? Will you need to add anything or take away? Will it need a motor and if so, where best should you install it? and so forth.

In this way, your child has created a project – creative in itself – but you have now introduced a problem (or let's call it a new design spec) which arouses curiosity, presents an opportunity to think about the possibilities, evaluate ideas and then come up with a solution.

Innovative and critical thinking

To help your child develop critical thinking, encourage them to think about new and original ideas. For example, after a family movie, you can ask, 'What do you think we can learn from this movie?' Or perhaps ask why they think a character behaved in a certain way. You can also ask how they would change the ending to make it happier/sadder/more exciting.

This type of questioning also lends itself well to story books. You could have all sorts of fun with 'How would the stories differ if Harry Potter or Alice in Wonderland were baddies?'

Creativity is not limited to the arts; creative people have an ability to adapt to a situation or come up with an innovative solution to a problem, often by rehearsing in their mind different imagined situations and outcomes. This is as true of the engineer or inventor as it is of the film director or actor. It's all about being able to explore the 'what if's?' that guide the creative process, and it is an essential entrepreneurial skill.

The question 'Can you imagine?' is an excellent prompt to your child to think innovatively. Give your own imagination free rein, but also think about topics that interest your child and see what interesting questions you and your child can come up with.

Can you imagine what life would be like if we had flying cars? Would we need traffic lights and where would we put them? How would you prevent mid-air collisions?

If you could build a robot, what jobs would you have it perform? What skills would it need to be able to perform those jobs? Would it be easier to build a robot that could open doors or a house that didn't have any?

Simple DIY projects present ideal opportunities to nurture innovative and creative thinking. For example, when fixing things around the home ask your child whether they can come up with suggestions as to how it can be fixed. There are different ways of fixing an item and you need to persevere in finding the right solution to the problem. Traditional construction kits are great, whether primarily designed to create one thing, with instructions provided, or the old fashioned assortment of bits and pieces, gears and wheels etc. that would positively encourage you to give your imagination free rein. There are some great kits out there, many of which are reviewed on the Enterprising Child website.

WHAT YOUR CHILD IS LEARNING

These activities focus on the creative process - arousing curiosity, perceiving possibilities, evaluating problems and coming up with solutions, testing and adapting, so that your child is honing their ability to develop critical, creative and innovative thinking.

Creativity is an essential part of the entrepreneurial character, whether creating a business, inventing a new product or simply finding a way to do things better. It engages and develops a wide range of entrepreneurial characteristics. Imagination is needed to perceive and reflect upon possibilities, ambition and tenacity to get stuck in and persevere in the face of setbacks, judgments of value are called into play in finding the best way to do things and, although we sometimes think of creativity as a solitary pursuit, there is always a social dimension – we create for an audience (or market) and often in cooperation and building on the work of others.

The business of money

Following on from activities to help younger children understand the concept of buying and selling, saving or spending, you can now begin to introduce more practical activities to help older children understand how to manage money and explore how monetary value is determined.

Not only do children need to learn that goods and services all cost money in some form, they also need at least a basic understanding of managing cash, banking, saving and investing, including technology, such as ATM machines, debit and credit cards, and online banking.

Beyond these basic life skills, preparing children for the world of commerce and enterprise and developing their entrepreneurial characteristics means providing opportunities to explore the nature of these enterprises, which are as much a feature of our world and which require as much understanding and literacy as any other aspect of the social or natural world.

ACTIVITIES

The price is right

The object of this game, based on the TV quiz show of the 1980s, is to guess the price of an object. It's not necessary to sit in a room with the objects placed in front of you – it's just as much fun moving from room to room, placing a price on any object you choose. All you need is a pen and some sticky post-it notes.

The game can also be played with an old store catalogue. Use a thick black marker to blot out the price of each product and have your child guess the price.

This is not an opportunity to lecture your child on how expensive their toys are, but to help them begin to understand the notion of relative value and pricing. It will also help your child to appreciate that we need to be careful with possessions, as possessions cost money to replace.

Discuss with your child why certain items cost so much and others considerably less. For example, solid wood might be more expensive than plastic. Something which has been handmade might be more expensive because of the manual labour involved, and so on. These are factors which contribute towards the pricing of products.

Setting up shop

As well as discussing the price of goods you might also like to explore the relationship between the shop and the manufacturer or wholesaler. Small children generally love playing shops, but with children of this age you can extend the game to include trips to the wholesaler or orders from the manufacturer, keeping a record of the prices paid for goods against sales income so that they can explore the notion of profit or loss. You can do this for real with the traditional lemonade stall or extending the activities in the 4-6 age group (*Selling it like it is*) such as picking up bargains at car boot sales to sell on, only this time with more emphasis upon the numbers and the need to control costs, maximise sales and make a profit.

There are a host of absorbing and educational on-line games which explore these issues, including simulations of the traditional lemonade stall as well as business board games. Reviews and links are available on the Enterprising Child website.

Consumer test

Children are susceptible to the subtle advertising messages surrounding brands – whether it is for shoes, clothes, trainers, toys or food. Help them to appreciate that while there might be several different brands of a particular product, in many cases a comparison between the brands may show that there is little or no difference.

This is a comparison game, so probably best suited to everyday items such as groceries. Whenever you do your weekly or monthly shop, select a brand product and a supermarket basic product or two different brands.

Cover the labels, mark one item 'A' and the other 'B' then ask your child to compare brands. Is there any difference in taste? Have them make a note in a notepad, just like a real consumer test. Having your child test the product in this way is far more effective than trying to explain why you won't buy Brand 'X' over another.

Do point out, however, that purchases are often based on quality or value, not just cost, so while some items may be cheaper, they may not be better value. Also, some purchases are made according to ethical, e.g. fair-trade, considerations or to support local business such as the greengrocer or butcher, where, although prices may be a little higher, the decision to shop local is made in the light of values which you can certainly discuss with your children.

As well as developing your child's discernment as a consumer, these considerations of brand and pricing also help to reinforce a very valuable entrepreneurial lesson, that the price of an item or service is not governed solely by the cost of production or rarity of that item but also by what people are prepared to pay for it, its' perceived value, and that this may rely upon lots of subjective factors (a great way to begin to explore and understand the mysteries of marketing).

Save, spend, share
While there are debates around whether children should be given an allowance or whether they should 'earn' their pocket money, the fact is that encouraging your child to manage cash and manage it well, is an important skill for life. Your child's piggy bank does not have to be the traditional little pink pig and they can have more than one.

Take three attractively decorated jars, and label them:

* SAVE
* SPEND
* SHARE

Encourage your child to divide their allowance or pocket money into the three jars.

SAVE is for investing, or saving up for more expensive items. Encourage your child to think long-term. When appropriate, this can be put into a savings account.

SPEND is for smaller items such as weekly pocket money purchases. When appropriate, you can open a young person's bank account.

SHARE is for charitable giving. Discuss the importance of helping others who are less fortunate than them and help your child to choose a charity that interests them by doing some research on the internet or by locating local charities. Have a discussion around whether they would like to divide their money equally among the three jars or whether they would like to apportion different percentages. This is also a good opportunity for you to share your own ways of saving, spending, and sharing.

The hole in the wall and the bottomless pocket

> *(We) are very passionate about ensuring we don't bring up children who are spoilt, and Kayla has seen us both working so understands that much of what we have, such as a nice house, cars and so on, are achieved by working really hard; there's no*

shortcut. My heart sank the other day when we went into a well-known department store to discover that Monopoly now has a credit card included in the game, I mean what's that teaching children?

Tim Campbell MBE, dad to Kayla (11) and Aaron (2)

Some children do not realise that you cannot take money out of your bank account, unless you first put money into it; they think that you simply tap some numbers into the hole in the wall and it dispenses money whenever you need it.

The next time you take money from the cash dispenser, ask your child whether they know how the money gets there.

If they are earning pocket money, you could use the analogy of their own piggy bank funds that they have had to earn in order to be able to deposit it, before they can take anything out.

Some banks have cash clubs, to help children get to grips with managing money, many of which can be opened with as little as £1, with incentives such as rewards which can be collected and redeemed for prizes and interest.

Whilst you are discussing how money gets into your bank account, it might also be useful to explore the relationship between prices and income beyond your child's experience of managing their own pocket money. Children can fairly easily grasp that something costing £100 is more expensive than something costing £1 (as in the *Price is Right* game), but these price comparisons need to be related to notions of affordability; it is here that children often struggle and believe that the parental pockets are bottomless. Whilst 'Money doesn't grow on trees' is a well-worn response to children's unrealistic expectations of affordability, it has little value as an economic model that gives children any kind of inkling of where the family's money does come from and how that relates to purchases.

It's not necessary to discuss the contents of your pay packet, in fact it would probably be counterproductive – even the minimum wage would sound like a massive amount of money to a child used to dealing in pocket money amounts, but simple arithmetical puzzles along the lines of *Mr Jones earns £400 pounds a week and spends £150 per week on rent, £120 per week on food and groceries and so on... how many computer games can he buy with what's left if each game cost £20 each?* would start to get the message across. You can even get your child thinking about costs relative to income by making a game of whether they can identify all the things that the family has to pay for in a month.

It's a matter of choice
Encourage a degree of independence by allowing your child to make their own decisions with their own money. However, do point out that there are consequences and contingencies associated with purchase decisions. For example, if they decide they want a new scooter, do they have enough money to buy it? If not, how will they pay for it? If they are earning pocket money, how long will it be before they can afford to earn enough to buy it? What might they need to forego in order to make this purchase?

Discuss with your child that managing money responsibly is also about deciding responsibly. This is a good opportunity to discuss the difference between needs and wants. While it is not wrong to treat themselves occasionally, in some cases needs should take priority over your wants. Additionally, if they cannot afford to buy something, then rather than borrow the money it might be better to wait and save up for it.

A fun game to play with your child to help teach this lesson is *Needs versus wants*. As you walk around the shops, encourage your child to make a list of items which they think are needs and another which they think are wants. Back at home, discuss with your child what is on the list. Do they understand why items such as toys, games, CDs, DVDs and sweets are not needs, and are they able to make a rational case for inclusion of an item in one category or the other? This can be a helpful way of applying cognitive approaches to desire, thinking things through as opposed to acting on impulse. It is also a way of introducing philosophical reflection and the notion of a hierarchy of needs – your child may even be able to reflect upon the fact that there are needs (for fun, social contact, self-esteem) that are met by things which are not needs in themselves; for example it is arguable that children need stuff to play with as part of their healthy development, even if they don't need any particular toy. Much marketing works on blurring these distinctions to create an experience of need in the creation of wants.

Your work

Discuss with your child how products or services are priced in your line of work. If a service, are people paid hourly or by the project? If you sell products, how are items priced? How are people persuaded to buy what is being sold? Are your products and services something that people need or just something they want?

WHAT YOUR CHILD IS LEARNING

Earning, saving, spending, giving away and managing money is a part of everyday life. Inevitably, there are costs associated with running a business or in the workplace. It's important to understand that the buying of services or goods cost money, as do the providing of services and goods. Efficiently budgeting and managing cash flow is crucial to the success of any business.

In order to create a product, materials need to be bought and machinery needs to be bought or leased. Staff, whether freelance or on the payroll need to be paid. Experts need to be hired for tax and accountancy purposes. There often seems to be an endless list of costs associated with running a business, so developing an ability to make sensible choices in business could mean the difference between a healthy profit, a loss or even bankruptcy.

The Spend, Save, Share lesson is a familiar one in business, that while there are costs associated with running a business, there is also a need to invest back into it to enable it to grow and indeed to invest in the communities which the business is serving. The activities in this section will also help to provide further grounding for your child in developing a critical understanding of the nature and context of business life and the beginnings of a vocabulary and cognitive skills for discussing and making decisions on issues around price, cost, profit, brand, value, business ethics, and other essential features of life in the 21st century.

Ambition and Aspirations – you can get it (if you *really* want)

Enterprising people have a game plan; they have a picture of what they want to achieve in the long term, and an idea of the steps they need to take to get there.

To give your child a head start in life you can encourage them to develop their ability to formulate a game plan by supporting them to set and meet appropriate challenges.

Formulating a goal, imagining what it will look or feel like to achieve that goal, making it tangible and specific, helps in the act of working towards that goal, providing both motivation and the means to identify necessary steps or sub-goals. It will also encourage your child to look forward, to aspire and make it more likely that they will succeed.

The entrepreneurial individual is a self-starter; they set their own goals and plan how they will achieve these goals, so encouraging your child to set personal goals for themselves will help them develop self-motivation and self-belief. As parent you can help your child set goals that are both achievable but also stretching so that they get the positive reinforcement of having achieved something, but something that was a challenge they accepted and met.

ACTIVITIES

50 things to do before you're 11 ¾

The National Trust run an initiative called *50 Things to do before you're 11 ¾*, designed to encourage children to explore the great outdoors[59]. You will need to register your child's name online and activate the account, but after that they are free to use the site to log their own activities and record their attainment of specific goals.

Daily activities are grouped into main headings which should

---

[59]www.50things.org.uk

appeal to different types of personalities. So, for example, under the heading 'Adventurer' activities such as tree climbing, rolling down a really big hill, and building a den are included. Under 'Discoverer' there are activities such as making a mud pie or hunting for treasure on the beach. These are all fun, and make the whole idea of goal setting enjoyable and not intimidating.

Fun To Do list
You probably use a To Do list yourself and no doubt your child has seen you post this somewhere like the fridge or computer. Encourage children in the upper age range to set more challenging goals for themselves using the principle of a To Do list, but adapted to make it fun.

The idea is to make a list of things your child can accomplish by themselves. Depending on their ability, you can consider setting a time period – perhaps 'Seven things I would like to do in 21 days.'

Explain that it is a good idea to set ourselves goals which are slightly challenging, as this helps us improve. Talk about things you always wanted to do as a child and, with help, managed to get done. Alternatively, if there was something you always wanted to do as a child, but never got round to accomplishing, discuss that too.

If you are agreeing a time limit, your child might initially suggest unrealistic goals for the period, but this will still give you insights into what they want, what excites them or even what they fear. All of these provide clues about their motivation. What they would like to achieve could be made into a more suitable longer-term goal, in which case you could encourage them to think about intermediate steps or identifiable sub-goals. The main thing is to work with what motivates your child, to encourage them to dream, but also to make their dreams realisable by identifying the route to success and setting markers along the way.

The following is an example of a 14 day To Do list made by Alexander, aged 11. Alexander has Asperger's as well as mild co-ordination problems, so his original goals were amended to longer term goals, (those marked with an asterisk) and changed to the alternative 14 day challenge in brackets:

1. Overcome my fear of escalators* (go up the short escalators at the library once)
2. Write three different short stories – an adventure, a mystery and a comedy
3. Learn how to ride a bike* (steady myself twice, without falling off)
4. Make an Eiffel Tower structure out of Connex construction kit
5. Reach 50 kick-ups

Once they've made the list, discuss the challenge together and decide if anything needs a plan of action to be drawn up, so that your child knows what steps they need to take. Be supportive throughout, offer advice with any items which your child might find particularly challenging and encourage them to stick with it. At the end of their challenge, make a big fuss of celebrating their success and then plan the next challenge.

Soila Sindiyo, a single mother of two girls, encourages her daughters to be ambitious by helping them to aim higher soon after each goal has been met.

When they achieve a certain goal, I make a point to acknowledge it together with them and depending on what it was we celebrate it. Once this goal has been achieved then the posts almost immediately move further on and a new bigger goal is set.

I try and get them to understand that if they have done very well, it's great, but that means they can do even better.

It's *very* important to teach your child to not fear failure. It is ok for them to fail in achieving a goal, since this provides valuable feedback which will increase their opportunity for learning and chances of success in the future. The important thing is to encourage them to see 'failure' as an opportunity for learning – to pick themselves up, reflect and move on. Ask them to think about how they might improve next time round: was the goal unrealistic or not fully formulated, imagined or thought through, or do the steps to success need to be adjusted so that they tackle things differently next time around? Is this something they really want or something they think they should want?

Failure teaches us to plan better and good planning is a major key to future success. Fear of failure, as opposed to a desire to succeed, is the mortal enemy of enterprise and a real barrier to developing adaptability and the capacity to adapt to the novel circumstances and moving goal posts which fast paced technological and economic change creates.

Be well 'travelled'

Thanks to the internet, the world is a smaller place. We can be well 'travelled' without leaving the home. For example, travelling to the corners of the world via Google Earth can be good fun, as can borrowing some inspirational books from the library. *Soila Sindiyo* illustrates how she does this with her younger daughter, aged seven.

> *We travel via books, YouTube and the internet. This is opening my daughter's eyes. My seven year old used to speak of going to the University of India, loves Bollywood dancing and thinks she has to learn to eat chillies in preparation for India. We haven't even been to India.*
>
> *Spain is taking over because she is doing flamenco dancing. YouTube flamenco dancers have helped whet her appetite. Her world is much smaller than mine ever was. I would like her to know that she can go anyway, when she wants and chooses to.*

Travel, whether in the mind or physically, is a great way of developing imagination and ambition, opening the mind to new horizons, and stimulating the desire to reach beyond one's own circumstances and surroundings. The metaphor of the journey provides a natural framework within which to consider issues of goal setting, planning, and keeping on track.

WHAT YOUR CHILD IS LEARNING

Entrepreneurs are naturally ambitious people; they perceive the possibility of achieving a particular goal, recognise its value, and plan how to reach it.

There are several important things that your child is learning and experiencing through the activities above; validation of their capacity to dream and to imagine new futures in as much detail as they can, recognising the need to plan and identify the steps to success, dealing with failure and feedback from the environment, and learning to recognise and celebrate the successes along the way that form part of a larger plan, and thus keep themselves motivated. All of these are essential elements of the enterprising lifestyle and a sure foundation for contributing to the realising of value in life, business, or the workplace.

Interview with Laura Tenison MBE, founder and CEO of *JoJo Maman Bébé*

LAURA TENISON MBE is founder and Managing Director of maternity and baby company JoJo Maman Bébé. In 2012 her company has a gross turnover of £31 million and employs 400+ staff in 46 stores around Britain. The business is growing organically, year on year. Laura has a strong work ethic (famously once putting in 18 hour working days while building the business), somehow finding time to give talks on female entrepreneurialism, help run a children's charity fighting infant mortality in Mozambique, mentor young entrepreneurs, take on work experience students and yet ensure she is there for her family.

LAURA, YOU WERE IN MANY RESPECTS AN ENTREPRENEURIAL CHILD, DESIGNING, MAKING AND SELLING CLOTHES IN YOUR TEENS. HOW DO YOU FEEL YOUR PARENTS INFLUENCED YOUR DECISIONS ABOUT WORK?

My parents took little interest in my entrepreneurial spirit, but they did like me being productive and my mother certainly instilled a good work ethic into us. When, as a child, I found an interest in sewing, they encouraged me by giving me a sewing machine as a birthday present and the fabrics I needed for my hobby. I grew up in the countryside and had to make my own entertainment.

My parents were quite frugal and pocket money was kept to a minimum. Finding ways to supplement the cash was a constant source of entertainment. My brothers and I would try anything to earn a little holiday money; from picking fruit to selling strawberries on the main road or making cakes to sell to neighbours.

Whilst my parents were encouraging with our activities, they were quite surprised and concerned when I decided to turn my dressmaking 'hobby' into a way to earn a living – they would have preferred me to get a 'proper job'. So whilst my parents did not actively encourage me to start my own business, my mother's attitude to money and her instilling its value into me from a young age, has been hugely beneficial.

HOW DO YOU FEEL WE AS PARENTS CAN ENCOURAGE OUR CHILDREN TO HAVE A SIMILAR WORK ETHIC – OF NOT EXPECTING THINGS TO BE HANDED ON A PLATTER, SO TO SPEAK? WHAT TOP TIPS MIGHT YOU HAVE FOR OTHER PARENTS KEEN TO NURTURE A GOOD WORK ETHIC?

I fully believe that not being spoilt is no bad thing. This is much harder nowadays when consumer spending is rife and peer pressure for our children to have the latest look can be demanding. I am not nearly as strict with my children as my parents were with us, simply because I do not want them to be ostracised, but I do try to encourage them to budget and save for things they really want.

I encourage them to earn a little pocket money by doing chores around the house. Taking a Saturday job or doing a small business will hold them in good stead when it comes to running their finances in the future or even on the job market. I would far rather employ a graduate who has a proven work ethic than one who has been travelling around the world on his or her parents' credit cards.

THE VALUE OF MONEY:

My advice is to start teaching children how to deal with money from a young age. Pocket money could be given from a young age – as early as five years upwards. The amount could, for example, start at a low basic which could be taken away as a form of sanction. It could also be increased if certain household chores are undertaken without complaint, for example clearing the table, sorting out bedrooms, folding the laundry etc. Each child should then be given a money box and a purse and the pocket money should be divided equally between the two. The purse is for spending – frivolous purchases such as sweets or comics whereas the money box could be a savings bank for the future.

It is a good idea to have a savings goal. Children are more likely to put more money into the savings bank if they have a reason. So if they are saving up for a computer game and you work through the level they need to save each week to achieve their goal quicker – they may decide not to spend half their money on sweets! It's a pretty simple idea, but it is amazing how few people believe in pocket money these days. Simply handing out cash on demand sets a really bad precedent.

ENTREPRENEURSHIP:

I am not at all sure you can teach entrepreneurship. Some children really want to start businesses and others just want to chat to their friends. It can be lonely running a business as a child, especially one which requires time and dedication which all has to be fitted around school and sports fixtures, leaving very little time for play. But those who are keen to earn their own money might like try some of the following simple business ideas to get them started:

1. *Simple trading – one man's junk is another man's treasure. CDs, video games, books and clothes are all easy to pass on to friends for a knock down price.*

2. *Baking to order – bake some gorgeous cakes together with your children, which you can sell to the neighbours on a Friday night. They need to look and taste great and with any luck you can get regular orders from family and friends.*
3. *Flower deliveries – take your children with you to a wholesale florist and buy up a stock of lovely flowers. Divide them up and wrap them artistically with brown paper and raffia bows. Offer them to the neighbours at a mark-up and suggest a weekly delivery.*
4. *Every adult appreciates help with cleaning and sweeping, possibly sorting out the shed or hosing out the wheelie bins. Help your child to make a short, clear leaflet stating that you are happy to help with some chores, but don't state an hourly rate – suggest that you work for an hour and they should give you what they feel it is worth. This way you may well get paid for the effort you put in at a higher level than expected. This might need to be restricted to family and friends that you know well, or alternatively, it might be something that time permitting you do together during half-terms or the summer holidays.*
5. *Music upload service – Help your child to set up a local service offering to upload CDs, vinyls or tapes to an iPad or computer or ask your clients for their play list and register them with Spotify. Charge by number of uploaded tracks. Print leaflets and hand out to parents at the junior school gate. Make sure they see your children in uniform so they know you are serious and offer to do the work at their homes so that they do not need to give you their PCs to take away.*
6. *DON'T FORGET – the franchise model for business. If your local service in the street works well don't just stop there. Your business may not be scalable by you but you have the knowledge to train up your friends to do the same thing in their street, selling their product or service to friends and family. You may*

wish to keep the business under your name and umbrella giving your friends all the training and support they need (plus the stock in the case of the flowers or other delivery ideas). These business ideas are all great for scaling up!

Obviously it makes sense that no child should put themselves into a vulnerable situation and parents should make sure their children are working with friends or neighbours. It is also important to ensure your child does not get carried away with simply making money. It is very tempting to rank the business venture ahead of academic studies as I did throughout my childhood. Everything must be done in moderation.

Activities for children aged 11-14 years

Purposeful presentations

Setting their sights on sales

Creativity and the art of motivation

Keeping the lines of communication open

Developing leadership potential

Nifty networking

Giving it back and making their mark

Purposeful presentations

The 9-11 years *Team fun, team challenge* activities looked at how effective communication helps team members work together to meet a common goal. Earlier years *Let me entertain you* activities saw how story telling is used in business as a way to inspire and motivate others. The art of effective communication combined with storytelling can be built upon here to introduce the concept of making presentations. It helps that this age group's cognitive development allows them to understand more abstract thoughts and complex issues and to be able to consider things more logically.

Presentations are commonly used in business to introduce a new product or service in a creative way. Many sectors rely upon pictorial presentations, for example a story board for creative and media industries. In other industries it might be a speaker who also uses multimedia to help get key messages across.

Whatever method is used, being able to stand up in front of an audience and articulate a subject, thoughts and ideas confidently and clearly is a wonderful skill to have. Good presentation skills are often required by employers and as a business owner are crucial for engaging and securing potential clients, customers, and investors.

ACTIVITIES

Say it out loud
Reading aloud is a simple yet effective way to encourage the art of confident speaking. Encourage your child to read aloud to you, to read with emphasis and practise using pitch and pace. Listening to the way storytellers tell stories is a good way of helping them see how others make a story sound exciting; your local library should have a supply of audio books for all age ranges. Making good presentations is about feeling relaxed, confident, enthused – which in turn will have listeners excited and enthused.

Storyboard

To create a storyboard, first discuss ideas for the story, characters, and the theme of the story. Collect cuttings from newspapers and magazines. How will the story be best presented? Encourage your child to present their ideas in a logical way so that the story flows. For younger children in this age group, the storyboard might be a single strip, as in a comic strip. For teens, this might be a longer storyboard – let their personal ability be your guide. They can write in a sentence or two within the story board as prompts, but the idea is for it to consist mainly of pictures.

The idea of this exercise is to help them see that different types of presentation – depending on their end use – require different methods, in this case mainly pictorial.

Be a TV presenter

Encourage your child to pick a subject and prepare a presentation on it. To differentiate this from the sort of activity your child might be asked to take part in at school, you can firstly ensure that they know that they can pick any subject, including one of their own private passions (e.g. a particular computer game, TV show, or football team), and secondly let them know that you are going to record it so that you can watch it as a 'TV programme' later. Most children will love the idea of being a TV presenter, and the fact that they can watch a play back of their 'programme' means that you will be relieved of the odious role of critic when it comes to the quality of their presentation; your child will be able to see for themselves whether they are mumbling or speaking too quietly, filling in with 'um' and 'you know' and will be motivated to do better.

Make it clear that they can do as many takes as they like before the 'programme' is added to the family TV archive (it could be the first of many!) and this will encourage them to refine their performance. Be positive and gives lots of praise, it is not your role to criticise but to cheer-lead; you can rely upon them to do their own self-criticism in this context.

Encourage your child to do their own research, write up their own notes then present their programme in any way they feel appropriate, for example, using PowerPoint or drawing illustrations on paper.

You can take this a step further by asking questions either throughout their presentation or at the end of it, becoming the 'live studio audience' questioning the celebrity presenter. The lesson learned here is in the whole process of researching, preparing and presenting the subject matter.

About turn

A fun exercise for this age group is to debate on a subject of their choosing. It may be an important social or ethical issue, but, as this is meant as a fun family exercise rather than the sort of debating they might do at school, you can encourage them to select a subject such as 'Why we shouldn't have to eat our greens' or 'Why we shouldn't have to go to school'. They initially argue for their case, until you interject with the phrase 'about turn', at which point they then have to argue against it.

It's a fun, light-hearted way to practice mental agility, the usefulness of which will not be lost on your child in later life when they are quizzed during an interview or if they ever have to pitch to investors.

WHAT YOUR CHILD IS LEARNING

Effective leaders and entrepreneurs are *influencers* – they know how to get their point across persuasively, in a succinct but also engaging and enthusiastic manner, whether it be a sales pitch, a bid for investment, or a rallying of the team to get a job done or maintain morale in turbulent times.

The activities above are intended to help your child master the art of confident speaking, of being able to articulate their point in a way that others can understand. With your support and encouragement, the activities will help your child build their self-confidence and become more aware of how to use verbal and non-verbal communication skills to best effect.

Setting their sights on sales

I think (Kayla's) horizons of considering what is possible are significantly broader than mine were at that age... and I can see how the way in which we influence her is manifesting itself – at just 11 years old Kayla is very focused on 'Well, why can't I make something to sell or do something to get the money for what I want' rather than just saying 'I want that'.

Tim Campbell MBE, dad to Kayla (11) and Aaron (2)

Building on the activities in Rate the Sale within the 6-9 age group, and *The Business of money* in 9–11 years, as your child enters their teens you can involve them in more sophisticated examples of buying and selling activities. They can, for example, learn more about the role of advertising, marketing and how supply and demand is connected with those roles, as well as more about profit, loss, financial management and investment.

These activities can be used to encourage your child to start mini enterprising projects to familiarise them with how the world of commerce and enterprise operate. Work with your child to discuss their experiences, noticing which areas they excel at and which they are more challenged by, for example whether they are a natural sales person or more of a planner or financial manager.

Their projects can be used to generate real interest within their community or among their friends, and can be an exciting first taste of what real business is all about.

The activities below are not presented as a comprehensive guide to setting up a business, (there are many useful introductory texts on this, detailed on the Enterprising Child website) but are provided as ways to help encourage your child to become more familiar with some of the key tasks and concepts of running their own business, which will stand them in good stead whether or not they eventually go on to be a business owner or an employee.

Fun with advertising

Advertisements are part of everyday life, but does your child know why companies advertise? For the younger child within this age range, point out adverts in magazines or newspapers. Discuss what makes up an advertisement, the catchy slogans or taglines, the persuasive copy, the price, who the advert is intended for.

As a fun activity, when you are watching a television programme or family film together, see how many adverts they can count throughout the course of the film each time there is a break. Notice the type of advertisements being broadcast and discuss who they think these are aimed at. For example, are they aimed at women, men, parents or children? How are the advertisers attempting to sell the product, what is the underlying message that they want to convey to audiences to persuade them to buy the product? You can record adverts for playback later, so your child can analyse them in a more frame by frame way.

Children in the upper age range can get involved in creating an advert – perhaps for a favourite item of theirs. Using an advert from a magazine as a template, see what elements of this advert they can copy. What catchy slogan will they use for the heading? Who is the target audience? What are the benefits and main features of this product? What will be the price? Look in local newspapers for competitions encouraging children to for example design a poster for an event.

This activity opens up an opportunity to discuss how companies get their message across to prospective customers as well as existing ones. How will they market their product – through traditional print advertising, online, social media, or a combination of these? How does a message need to be adapted in print versus online? How does the message differ when advertising to existing customers as opposed to prospective ones?

Discuss competitors and why they exist. So you might, for example, start by having your child identify different brands of the same item. Why do these different brands exist? Why is brand image so important to businesses?

Understanding advertising is important, not just because it will make your child a more discerning consumer, but also because you are introducing some of the fundamental concepts of marketing and, most importantly of all, getting across the message that products and services need customers who want, or can realistically be persuaded that they want, to purchase those products or services. This may seem an elementary message but it is a key business concept and fundamental to entrepreneurial success.

Fun with buying and selling: offline
The challenge in this activity is to explore whether your child can, within a limited budget, buy and sell items on at a profit. Let them find items from, say, a car boot sale, charity shops, or from friends (you might want to suggest a sale or return commission based option for selling friends unwanted items), or even from wholesalers and see what they can do.

Young entrepreneur *Jamie Dunn* did just this when he started secondary school and by the time he was 15 years old was earning up to £600 profit on a good day by selling CDs and DVDs sourced from a wholesaler.

Selling can be online (see the activity further on) or offline. The important thing is to encourage your child to become involved in all the elements outlined below, as that way they will get the most realistic and satisfying overall introduction to real enterprise. Take it a bit at a time if that works well for your child, rather than introducing all the elements in one go. The most important principle here, as always, is that they should feel a sense of ownership of the activity and that it is enjoyable and rewarding for them.

- *Planning* – Discuss which items will be sold and why, then decide upon a date and time. Next plan the advertising of the event (if organising it yourself) and discuss the link between advertising and selling. They may want to design some posters then discuss where best to place these; explain that this is part of the marketing plan which summarises how your child can reach their prospective customers so that they know what is on offer and are motivated to find out more.
- *Finance*[60] – It's very important that your child gets into the habit of recording all the relevant financial details in a way that makes it easy for them to keep track of costs and income. You can use simple accounts software for this or it may be clearer to start using a notebook with a page to record the 'balance sheet' (for the purpose of this activity that would just be where the initial allowance you give them is recorded), a page to note purchases apart from stock to sell (overheads – e.g. the fee to enter a car boot sale, any advertising costs), a page to record 'cost of sales' (what the goods your child is selling actually cost to purchase), a page to record income from sales, and finally a page to summarise general expenses, cost of sales, sales income and gross profit (sales less cost of sales) and finally the net profit or loss (sales less cost of sales less expenses).

  Discuss what price they will sell each item for and why. What

[60]Basic accounts sheets with notes are available to download from the Enterprising Child web site

are people prepared to pay for second-hand items? This opens up a discussion as to what process goes into pricing an item, including its cost (to produce or purchase) and what people are prepared to pay for it – generally market conditions, the level of demand for a particular item or type of item, the supply available (how many others are being sold by competitors) and the general state of the market (how much money people have to spend and how inclined they are to spend it, which will also influence factors such as the relative popularity of second hand as opposed to new toys, for example). Of course the main thing is to make a profit; there's no point in selling all their items at a loss, although you may want to think about whether a loss leader (an item sold at a loss or minimal profit to attract trade and increase overall sales and profit) would be useful at some stage.

Discuss which items are likely to sell for more, such as CDs, popular games or toys. This opens up the discussion around consumer behaviour.

On the actual day, encourage your child to handle the cash, as this is an excellent opportunity for them to practise counting the correct change and writing receipts.

- *Display* – How will items be arranged on the day? Will they be sold on a table and if so how will they be arranged? Discuss the whole buying process from the customer's point of view – items which are presented nicely stand a better chance of being viewed as worth the price. Clothes labelled 'Vintage' or 'Retro', or games labelled 'Classic', may sell better than those labelled simply 'used' or 'second-hand'.

- *Customer Service* – Understanding the buying process also encompasses how the customer is treated. Could they for example be offered a drink while they are waiting? It need only be plastic cups and a soft drink – but it helps to be perceived as important.

On the day itself, encourage your child to give their customers their full attention, to be courteous and friendly. The old adage *'customer is king'* is a good lesson to learn, even for youngsters. It's good to be welcoming so that your customers want to come back for more.

- *Employees* – Depending on how many items they have to sell, your child may have a friend who would like to help out on the day. This is an ideal opportunity to have a discussion about employees. What is an appropriate price to pay their friend for helping out? You will no doubt need to help them decide how much, but it's a good discussion to have. It's worth discussing the costs and benefits of employing staff in terms of overall profitability, this will help them better understand the quandaries faced by many businesses considering expansion or struggling to retain staff.

Jamie Dunn enlisted the help of his two unemployed sisters to help out with sourcing goods from wholesalers for his stall. He learned about more than just employing people:

Getting my sisters involved was important because I learned then that I didn't need to work too hard to earn money, I could get others to do that for me.

Fun with selling: online

The internet has made it possible to sell online regardless of location, opening up the opportunity for businesses to reach larger markets. As businesses increasingly see the need to have an online presence – indeed, many businesses are entirely online – equipping your child with an understanding of how online selling works will give them a very real and practical skill for life.

If they are not already involved, encourage your child to embrace the internet and use it to their advantage. Unwanted books, toys, mobile phones and clothes, as long as in a good condition, can be sold online. Take time to teach your child about internet safety and security[61]. It might be a good idea for you to let them trade care of you as their parent (a PayPal account can be set up for this purpose) though this is entirely dependent on their ability and your house rules. Here is what one parent had to say about their 13 year old son's use of the internet:

> *My son codes, he creates web sites, he is advanced at PhotoShop, he connects into talent communities online where he thinks he might like to work and he did a presentation in London the other day on what it's like to be an entrepreneur! He has asked if he can do his work experience at a company he's found in the U.S.A. His generation don't just look at what's available to them in their home town, they see the world as very small because they are connected with it continuously. He has overshot his teacher, my son learns everything he needs to know from Google and many others have too.*

Julie Bishop, mum to Paul (13)

It is likely that your child has developed a good understanding of how to use computers to navigate around the online world as this is included in the school curriculum. *Kris Clarke* is one such parent who has two daughters, one of whom is gifted and the other has dyslexia with temporal, phonological and auditory deficit. She quickly realised that their love of computers could be used to develop their entrepreneurial potential whilst dealing with their particular needs, so now at the ages of 10 and 14 they have both used their own strengths to create a website selling craft gifts supporting the work of other children with dyslexia.

---

[61]http://www.microsoft.com/security/family-safety/childsafety-age.aspx

The next steps

Valuable lessons can be learned for everyone involved in your child's initial experience of buying, and then selling, on or off line. The next step is to look carefully at the figures from this activity, for example what was the level of profit from the sale? If buying and selling was scaled up how would that translate into increased sales and profits?

If a loss was made, encourage your child to look at the reasons why rather than discourage them. Was the pricing wrong? Did they pay too much for the items they wanted to sell? Was the error in the marketing, presentation, or in the sales process? Were they trying to sell the wrong item in the wrong place?

There is so much that can be learned, and lots of interest and excitement in making plans to improve things next time round.

If your child's first business has made a profit you may want to take back your initial investment/allowance just as *Paul Lindley*, entrepreneur and founder of Ella's Kitchen, did with his children when he lent them a bucket and sponge to clean cars for the day.

Your child will need to learn about repaying investors and creditors if they do want to pursue business life in the future. Alternatively, you may want to let your investment stay in, in the hope that your child can use it to generate increased profit in the future.

Your child may just want to take all their profit (assuming they have made one) and spend it, but there is just the possibility that they have got the bug and will want to reinvest all or some of their profit in purchasing more stock to sell – they are then on the start of a very exciting journey indeed!

Beyond retail

These activities have focused on buying and selling, the basic retail model of business, but there is no reason why the same principles cannot be applied to a service or manufacturing model. If your child is gifted in creating arts, crafts, or even mechanical items, then they can produce and sell their own products and, essentially, will have a manufacturing business where the account keeping just needs to reflect a cost of manufacture – raw materials, and other overheads such as advertising, on-line selling fees or renting a table at, for example, a car boot or yard sale. It is probably best to exclude the cost of labour at this stage as this is likely to be only your child's own time, and they will soon work out if the profits being made are sufficient to 'pay' themselves anything and thus grasp the most important issue behind employment decisions.

Similar principles apply to a service business, for example your child might offer gardening services, car washing, website building and so on and here the business model is simpler again as there is nothing in the way of stock, only 'capital goods' such as the cost of a computer, or a bucket and sponge, and the usual overheads, including, for example, the cost of disposable items such as car shampoo.

Your work

If your work involves any aspect of the buying and selling process, including advertising and marketing, take some time to talk with your child about the process. What goes into the marketing aspect of the product or service? How do you advertise? Who closes the sale? Can you encourage them to come up with ideas about how to do things differently or better?

WHAT YOUR CHILD IS LEARNING

Buying and selling are at the heart of all entrepreneurial activity, not just in relation to the retail of goods, but because any business or social enterprise needs inputs as well as outputs, so there are costs as well as potential value to be realised.

In the activities above your child is encouraged to look at the process of actually running a business and this engages all of the characteristics identified as being present in the entrepreneur: they need to be able to perceive what is possible; see the opportunities that are there; engage their ambition and motivate themselves; assess risks and show resolve in getting out there and selling, either virtually or in the off-line world, whilst monitoring and pursuing their creation of value (in this case the realisation of a healthy profit margin and a satisfied customer base); utilising their teamwork and interpersonal skills in their dealings with suppliers, customers and possibly helpers/employees.

Creativity and the art of motivation

Entrepreneurs are people who have the ambition and motivation to create something of value. Motivation is an essential factor in creativity, in particular (although not exclusively) intrinsic motivation[62], being motivated by something they may be interested in or passionate about as opposed to extrinsic rewards such as money or fame. The creativity of entrepreneurs, and their level of intrinsic motivation, is one of their strongest characteristics; even when they have more than enough money, and could afford to spend the rest of their days relaxing, successful entrepreneurs tend to go on developing enterprises just because they have a passion to create.

For the entrepreneur extrinsic rewards are frequently late in coming – the individual who builds a successful business may themselves work far longer hours, for a relatively modest salary, than their employees in the earlier stages of the business, so if they were relying on extrinsic motivation alone they are unlikely to have the motivation to see the creation of successful new businesses as a reward in itself.

ACTIVITIES

Promote creative thinking

In establishing various techniques to nurture creativity in children, Nickerson[63] showed that one of the things educators need to do is identify what intrinsically motivates their students and then structure teaching around it. As a parent it is likewise good to get to know what motivates and inspires your child.

[62]Csikszentmihalyi, Mihaly (1990). Flow: The Psychology of Optimal Experience. New York: Harper and Row. ISBN 0-06-092043-2
[63]Nickerson, R. S. (1998). 'Enhancing creativity' in 'Handbook of Creativity' by Robert J Sternberg, PhD, Cambridge University Press. ISBN-13: 978-0521576048

As an example of what this means in practice, if your child shows an interest in painting then you might buy them the materials needed to take that interest further or perhaps borrow books from the library to help them perfect their technique, and so on.

The chances are that if you nurture your child's creativity in a passion or hobby they already show signs of interest in, they may well go on to pursue that interest further in later life. As parents we might prefer our child to pursue passions that are more likely to lead to material rewards, but generally a child that is encouraged to pursue their own calling is more likely to find a way of getting external rewards from that pursuit than one who is encouraged to simply follow the route of pursuing money or fame as an end in itself.

One of my passions was working with animals. When I said to my parents that I wanted to experience working with birds of prey my mother found a local falconry centre and booked me a day's course working with them. They encouraged me to volunteer some of my time to work at the centre... When finally I realised that I wanted to become a chocolatier and told my parents, they both said they would support me in whatever career I chose as long as it was what made me happy. They both then set about buying small amounts of equipment so I would have the tools to begin working with chocolate. My father helped me research chocolate suppliers and this led to him booking a three day training course at the chocolate Callebaut academy in Banbury, Oxford. They both gave up their time to join in and learn too.

Louis Barnett, young entrepreneur and founder of Chokolit

Pastime passions

Does your child enjoy tinkering or experimenting at home? This indicates an inquiring mind, in which case encourage them to learn a new skill, for example how to cook. Not only is this a practical skill, it can be thoroughly enjoyable and is the perfect outlet for experimenting with ingredients, flavours or indeed methods. You could have a budding chef who wants to apply scientific methods to cookery, just like Heston Blumenthal!

Jennifer Okpapi fell in love with the ingredients and spices of her country of origin, Nigeria. From a young age, she loved to experiment in the kitchen, so her parents encouraged her by allowing her to cook for family mealtimes. As she became more proficient, her confidence grew, enabling her to experiment even further with different spices, ingredients and methods. Jennifer later managed to gain funding for her business and turned her passion for food into the UK's first cookery school dedicated to African cuisine. Her cookery school now offers a range of day classes as well as its own range of food products.

Encourage your child to carry out simple DIY tasks around the home. There are all sorts of simple projects they can be entrusted with, such as fixing door hinges, hammering the nails back into a wooden fence, painting a wooden fence or gate, and so on.

Initially, carry out these tasks together so that they can watch how it is done, then allow them to continue by themselves. Perhaps resist the urge to watch over them, but allow them to continue working unsupervised. Simply encourage them to call upon you if they need help, but also assure them that you know they will do an excellent job. At all ages children love to feel trusted and will enjoy being able to carry out an adult task all by themselves.

The motivation here is primarily intrinsic as you are building upon an interest that already exists. Do be careful to ensure that the task is age appropriate and matches their skill and ability, so that they are not overwhelmed by the task.

If your child shows an interest in computers then they can be encouraged to 'look under the bonnet' by exploring either the hardware (it is possible for you to build a PC with your child for instance; instruction books are available that will guide you through this process), or by encouraging them to explore computer coding and programming – there is a real shortage of programming talent in the Western world, partly because IT education teaches children how to use software products rather than to experiment with developing their own.

When they are using or building upon a skill that they already have, you will find that your child is more likely to keep at it until the job is done and will be motivated to do the job well. They will have immense pride in their completed project.

WHAT YOUR CHILD IS LEARNING

Through these activities your child is developing a very practical life skill, the art of self-motivation, and experiencing the positive reinforcement of investing time and energy in skills development and creative effort through the satisfaction and pleasure they receive.

This should be no surprise to any parent who has watched their child persevere for hours at a computer game, purely for the creative satisfaction of mastering the requirements of the game. This capacity for serious, dedicated, exploratory play is what makes children so naturally entrepreneurial and needs to be cherished and encouraged.

Within the world of work, employers increasingly expect employees to use initiative and be trusted to work unsupervised, whether in an office environment or home working. Home based businesses are also very much the norm, indeed the majority of entrepreneurs will have started their idea from their home. So whether your child's future is to be a creator of businesses, a social entrepreneur or an employee, they will need to stay self-motivated and in touch with their passions if they are to succeed.

Keeping the lines of communication open

Make sure you have family time. It's easy when you grow up to spend more and more time with friends from school, but it's so important to keep that rapport with your family too. Family time is important, not just in terms of doing enterprising activities together but just being together, a walk in the park, a meal, simple things.

Adam Bradford, young entrepreneur and Director of UnITe Computing

Communication, and the ability to work within a team whether as team leader or team member, is an essential skill for an entrepreneur.

Encouraging your child to communicate effectively helps them to understand that other people have a point of view, and that each point of view needs to be respected.

When people feel their views are respected, they feel valued and this engenders trust. Where there is trust, there is a willingness to pull together as a team. Teamwork and open communication are, therefore, closely linked. So by encouraging your child to be a good communicator, you are laying the foundation for them to become a good team player.

During these activities, allow your child to express themselves, to listen, and to exchange ideas and develop the art of open communication.

ACTIVITIES
Let's talk
Family discussions can be a rewarding way to find out what is on everyone's mind and what's happened during the day, especially when relaxing or eating together. A regular family discussion, perhaps once a month, to discuss any issues your teen and other

family members are having helps to establish a culture of understanding and respect for others within the family. While you no doubt make yourself available to discuss issues with your child at any time of the day, having a regular time to discuss things together also sets a routine which can be comforting for them. These discussion times can be an opportunity to vent frustrations, set goals for the next month, or reflect on what has been good, not so good, and any learning from this. For children in the younger age range, a weekly discussion may be easier for them to remember what has happened during the previous week than the previous month.

Discussions could begin for example by asking 'Has the week/month been a good one for you?' 'What has been particularly good about it?' Take the time to reflect on all the positive things that have happened, and move on to anything less positive, discussing ways of addressing this. If it is an issue that has been raised at school, perhaps ask, 'Do you know who you can turn to at school to address this problem?' Rather than offer solutions or give advice, use this as an opportunity to encourage your child to find their own answers, to help them develop a sense of independence.

Encourage your child to discuss their goals for the next week or month. Review these goals at the next family discussion. This might be a nice time to share your own goals. It shows your child that goal setting doesn't stop when we become adults. Self-improvement is a continual process; when your child sees you setting and achieving your own goals, it provides an excellent example for them to follow.

The family that plays together...
The stresses of a fast-paced life can mean playing together is often relegated to bank holidays, half terms or the annual family holiday. As your child reaches the higher range of this age group they are more likely to place importance on relationships with friends than

with family, yet something wonderful happens when the family plays together. Everyone is relaxed, they lighten up and communication becomes easier, as *Martin Rowland*, single father of two girls explains:

One of our favourite games is where the three of us will sit facing each other. We write the name of a celebrity on a post-it note, stick it on each other's foreheads and the aim of the game is to guess who the celebrity is. The person guessing can ask questions, so that we can give clues. It's hilarious. On one occasion, we spent nearly two hours playing that simple game. My children have got Xbox, Wii and all sorts of other electronic games. They never spend two hours on those! We have so much fun with that simple game. Afterwards, we might go for a walk and have a really nice chat while we're walking.

Martin Rowland, single father of Jasmine (12) and Ellis (9)

Teachable moments

A teachable moment[64] can occur when something unplanned or unique happens, which engages your child's attention and lends itself to a discussion on that particular topic. The aim is to learn from that moment. These are wonderful opportunities to communicate with your child, and in many respects make it easier to open up sensitive or difficult topics. For example: it would be much easier to open up a discussion on telling lies if there was a news item regarding someone recently being jailed for corruption, or a discussion on the use of drugs, if someone has sadly died due to the misuse of them. When you make a mistake at home, talk through

[64]http://en.wikipedia.org/wiki/Teachable_moment

what has happened. How would they have handled this differently? Do they think you did the right thing? It's good to let your child see that you are not infallible.

These moments provide an excellent opportunity to listen to your child. Encourage them to talk, to give their opinion, think for themselves, and consider how they would come up with a solution if they were faced with a similar problem. Teach them how to listen and share your own views and opinions. This is about a mutual exchange of ideas, so you both need to listen to each other.

c u l8er lol

Texting is part of modern day life and teens have become very adept at it. However, there are concerns that it can encourage lazy writing, not to mention poor spelling. If your child is forever texting, encourage them to develop good writing skills through, for example, writing letters – whether by hand or on the computer. *Aquila* Magazine[65] for 8 – 13 year olds provides a safe *Pen Pal* page, where your child can exchange letters with others. If you have friends or relatives abroad, encourage your child to write to them occasionally, rather than hopping on to Skype. Letter writing will not only help them develop their actual writing skills but also express their thoughts at greater length than texting and tweeting alone allows. (However, whilst on the subject, it might be worth exploring with your child the communication and enterprising possibilities opened up by mobile technology and exploring the way in which they use and respond to text messages).

Another way in which children can be encouraged to develop good communication skills is through blogging; anyone can set up a blog for free and the act of writing one, especially if you know your friends will be able to see it, is a great way to develop your child's powers of expression and communication.

[65]Aquila Magazine www.aquila.co.uk

The only caveat would be the common sense one of looking at issues of anonymity and online safety. One valuable aspect of blogging is that if your child can secure an audience (this is by no means a given as far as the wider world is concerned, but there's no reason why family and friends can't access your child's blog) then blogging can become a positive, interactive experience as users respond to your child's posts and they can respond in turn. One example of a young person who has become a global sensation with her *Never Seconds* blog is 9 year old Scottish schoolgirl, Martha Payne[66].

Some schools have an intranet system, where homework is posted. Often, these include a facility which allows school children within the same class the ability to chat to each other online. This enables children, particularly the younger ones in this age group, to become familiar with typing and sending messages over the internet. You can encourage older children to email relatives or their friends, though monitoring their safe use of it and providing appropriate rules/guidelines[67] are important.

WHAT YOUR CHILD IS LEARNING

Being a good team player as well as an individual is what marks the difference between those who pursue a private passion without profit and those who can influence and work with others to create and bring something of value into the market place.

These activities are intended to help your child practise and develop their communications skills. This includes cultivating the capacity to be a good listener, understand and respect the views of others and the capacity to express their own thoughts effectively and persuasively.

---

[66]http://neverseconds.blogspot.co.uk/
[67]Microsoft Safety & Security Center http://www.microsoft.com/security/family-safety/

Developing leadership potential

Try to stand out from the crowd from as young an age as possible, don't just follow everyone else. I missed out on loads of opportunities because I thought it wasn't cool to speak up

Emily Cummins, young British inventor

Entrepreneurs are by nature leaders rather than followers; without the self-confidence to follow their own vision and the ability to inspire others they could not achieve their goals.

As your child enters their teens, they will face pressure from their peers to fit in and conform. While there are occasions where it may be appropriate to do this, it is important to help your child see the difference between confidently deciding for themselves what to do versus simply following the crowd. Your child first needs confidence to be able to make decisions independently of you then, building upon confidence, assertiveness and persuasiveness, to carry them through their decisions and take others with them.

ACTIVITIES
Confidence is king
Your child is now growing in maturity, but still needs help in gaining confidence – not to be mistaken with cockiness. Inner confidence is about having self belief, so do use as many opportunities as you can to compliment your child on a job well done. This can be when they have been creative, innovative or indeed when they show signs of displaying any of the very characteristics that we are encouraging you to help them develop.

Encourage them to tell you how they feel after they have achieved something – talk about and elaborate upon that feeling: make it real for them, recalling it with their senses and emotions as well as with their intellect so that it acts as an almost physical reminder of their achievements, reinforcing feelings of confidence and mastery.

You can also help them to become more confident by encouraging them to take on responsibilities where they need to make their own decisions. This might, for example, be asking them to do a small weekly shop for you. You could ask them to look through your cupboards, write a list of what they think you need and then do the shop for you (somewhere local to you). Perhaps only lend a minimal amount of support if they really need it, but the whole process will be a tremendous boost to their confidence.

Assertive not aggressive

A good leader is assertive, knows when to take charge of the situation, but is able to do so without being aggressive or controlling. You can help children develop this ability by encouraging them to speak up when they do not agree with something. Provide opportunities for open discussion in the home and encourage them to challenge you in a respectful way.

'Don't be afraid to say you don't agree with me on this. I won't mind! Let's discuss it together. What are your feelings on the matter?'

Being assertive also means respecting themselves, having the self-belief that they have something to offer of value, but also having the right to say no, respectfully. An environment in the home which enables open discussion will help them to develop this skill – one where each member is encouraged to express a differing point of view.

A good exercise to practise assertiveness is to encourage your child to take a step back, think about how they handled a situation, assess it, and then see how they can improve next time round.

So for example:

1. Write down a time when you felt you were taken for granted.
2. How did it make you feel?
3. How did you handle the situation?
4. What can you do to handle it better next time?

Encourage them to write this down, so that they can look back on it whenever they need to remind themselves what to do.

Passion and drive
There cannot be leadership without passion and drive – it is the force that compels leaders to keep going to reach their vision. Passion is highlighted in *Creativity and the art of motivation,* suggesting ways to nurture your child's intrinsic motivation with their existing hobbies or interests. Reinforce passion and vision in your child by encouraging them to talk about it often. When it becomes real in their mind's eye, it becomes something that they absolutely must follow through on, and they are more likely to carry others with them through the strength of their inner conviction.

Dealing with pressure
Teens are particularly susceptible to pressure from their peers, but confidence will enable your child to make a decision that may be right for them personally, but which might not necessarily be popular.

They can't be shielded from conflict and neither can you always be there to fix an issue for them. So do they know how to respond when faced with a dilemma? Role play is useful to work on ways of dealing with new social situations and pressures, especially when entering into their teens as they will inevitably come across new challenges they will not have faced in primary school. Using the power of imagination is helpful here; if they can visualise and experience it on a sensory level, they are more likely to be able to deal with a tricky situation confidently and effectively.

As highlighted in *Room for Growth*, children need a safe environment at home where they can test out ways of dealing with conflict and risk and confide their feelings of fallibility and insecurity; a safe haven free from pressure to achieve or conform. They need to be able to accept failure sometimes, reflect and then move on having learned from the experience with the parent providing positive and unconditional support.

Empathy and a respect for diversity

Empathy is more than having sympathy for someone. It is stepping into their shoes, having the ability to understand how they feel.

A good leader understands the differences in others and respects those differences. Give your child opportunities to show concern and consideration for others. Help them to recognise if they have been unkind – perhaps to siblings, friends or to you as a parent. Don't be afraid to say 'I felt hurt by your comment' or 'How would you have felt if someone did that to you?' Openly discuss feelings so that they recognise that feelings matter.

Encourage your child to give to others, for example through volunteering, where they can have hands on experience of helping others who are less fortunate than themselves. They can learn the importance of humility and compassion and not confuse self-confidence with arrogance and indifference to the difficulties that others may experience.

As discussed in the 6-9 age group *Giving it Back* activities, your child might draw inspiration from the example of others, even if in sad or tragic circumstances as in the case of *Harry Moseley*[68] or from stories such as *Chi-Mun Wong*[69]. These stories help your child to

---

[68]www.hhho.co.uk
[69]http://www.london2012.com/torch-relay/torchbearers/torchbearers=chi-mun-wong-988/

respect the strength and resolve of others, as well as feel inspired to act themselves.

Self-management

Good leaders are focused, determined and in most cases disciplined, which requires self-management. Help your child to proactively manage their time by encouraging them to use a calendar or planner; explore with them the benefits of deferring reward, e.g. looking at times when they have saved up for something rather than spending now.

Self-management also requires learning how to say 'no' on occasion. They can't please all of their friends all of the time, or be in three different places at the same time – especially if they have homework to complete and hand in the next day. They will need to learn how to prioritise what is more important and have the discipline (and courage) to relegate anything else to the bottom of the pile. In part, this comes back to applying those analytical habits of mind considered in *Stretch and Challenge* for 9-11 year olds, being able to step back from emotional pressures and the demands of others to assess the relative importance of demands upon their time. They need to assess the costs and benefits associated with performing or abstaining from any particular course of action.

WHAT YOUR CHILD IS LEARNING

A successful entrepreneur needs to have the self-confidence and courage to hold fast to their vision independently of the support or not of others; influencing the opinion of others rather than being influenced by them out of a desire to conform or follow. This does not mean that they will push forward blindly, ignoring all opinions but their own. They still need to asses risk and think things through, but they will have a secure framework of their own values and an inner confidence to do what they believe to be the right thing.

Not all judgments made by an entrepreneur will be good ones and they must have the humility and flexibility of mind to admit when they are wrong and accept responsibility for their decisions and the consequences.

The activities here are intended to help you as a parent work with your child to develop their personality and strengths so that they too can demonstrate leadership. This will involve helping them to have confidence in their judgments, but also a respect for facts and the importance of thinking things through in decision making. It also involves helping them to develop skills in managing and motivating themselves, and learning about the needs and concerns of others. Good leaders attract others prepared to follow them by good judgment, sound interpersonal skills and the courage and conviction to put seeking value above the pressure to conform. Helping your child along this demanding pathway is not an easy task, but one in which your own capacity for leadership (as opposed to authority) will be challenged and stretched.

Nifty networking

Entrepreneurs need to be good at networking, using opportunities for socialising and attending trade events to establish relationships with potential suppliers, customers, partners, investors, and collaborators. Traditionally this has been done face to face; increasingly, though, networking is also taking place online and specialist sites such as LinkedIn[70] have arisen for business and professional social networking. Leisure based sites such as Facebook and Twitter are also used have arisen for business, but that is a subject outside the scope of this book.

Learning to network effectively is a useful life skill; everyone needs friends, but we also can benefit from building a wider circle of contacts and people with whom we share mutual or reciprocal interests in work or in business.

ACTIVITIES

Notice the difference

Effective networking requires effective communication skills, essential for your child to get across to others their interests and requirements in an engaging way. Your child also needs to be able to *listen* and to show an interest in others through verbal and non-verbal means. *Active listening* describes a way of listening that includes the use of paraphrase, repetition and questioning to clarify what someone is telling you and encourage them to feel listened to and understood.

You can role play with your child to improve their social skills (being able to talk to the opposite sex can be a powerful motivator); take it in turns to be speaker and listener and notice the difference between your experience as a speaker when the listener uses non-verbal behaviour (body posture, gaze) and active listening to show interest, and your feelings when they deliberately start yawning, glancing at

[70]www.linkedin.com

their watch, fidgeting and looking away. This can be fun, but also a powerful way of enabling your child to grasp that there are simple but effective ways to improve the quality of their social interactions.

If your child learns the art of active listening, not only will they be able to build better relationships with others, but they will also get into the habit of attending carefully to what others are saying and so find it easier to assimilate useful information and recognise situations in which there are potential mutual interests or benefits to be explored.

Community focus

Communication and networking skills can also be learned and practised at local community events. *Katie*, aged 15, explains how her mum encouraged her to gain valuable social and communication skills.

> *Mum has encouraged me to become involved in community activities which have helped me to develop social and communication skills. I think this has helped me to become more independent and has also helped me greatly at school to work hard and be enthusiastic. Also I am not afraid to work with others within a group.*

Annie Manning, Katie's mum, explains which type of activities she encouraged Katie to participate in.

I have always encouraged (Katie) to be a team player by joining after school activities, including Beavers, ballet and sports. As a solo parent I have worked through most of the school holidays while Katie attended theatre and music workshops.

Katie has been coming to charity events for many years, helping with raffles and catering and producing posters for outings for the elderly.

She has also been involved with local elections helping me when I ran and other councillors and it was no surprise when she was elected for the school council herself.

She knows I will persuade her to try new things on a regular basis even the church barn dance which may not be seen as trendy was great fun nevertheless.

If you volunteer for a local charity, can your child help you with simple tasks or projects? They might be able to help organise a fund, help to raise sponsorship or run a stand.

Local events might offer opportunities for your child to be exposed to a diverse range of people who, for example, speak different languages, are differently abled or come from diverse cultures. This encourages your child to recognise and respect diversity and not to be thrown if future networking events bring them into contact with people with differences from their previous range of experiences.

Learning effective communication skills like the use of eye contact, facial expression and reading non-verbal cues can be more challenging for a child on the autistic spectrum, and they will probably require extra help in developing effective communication strategies. It is good for non spectrum children to have some awareness of these difficulties so that they do not misinterpret the behaviour of others, take offence or lose patience unnecessarily.

iSocialise

Online networking may be a familiar concept for your child and offers the potential for them to connect with a far wider range of people who share common interests from across the globe.

It can be more difficult to build real relationships or friendships on-line – humans rely heavily upon non-verbal communication: tone of voice, gesture, facial expression – to convey meaning and emotion and this is hard to replicate online. Emoticons or smileys are poor substitutes for non-verbal cues, and messages can be misinterpreted and intentions misread in the virtual environment. Having said this, the increased availability of broadband, software such as *Skype* and video-enabled chat rooms allow for calls and messaging with video images, so is already blurring the boundary between virtual and actual networking.

In the business world, social and training events are being attended, and real alliances and business relationships established at a distance, a trend that is likely to grow.

Safety on-line may be tricky in relation to social networking sites and your child. There is, sadly, online and off-line crime associated with social networking sites, much of which comes down to privacy and anonymity. Your child must be advised never to give away details such as their address, for instance, and ideally should avoid posting photos of themselves with any identifying details, or information about where they go to school and so on. By introducing them to safe practice at an age when you can monitor and supervise their social networking activity, you stand the best chance of helping your children gain the potential benefits without exposing them to risks. The advice from Microsoft[71] is to follow the general guidelines and requirements of social networking sites such as *Facebook* that the minimum age to be using it should be 13.

An example of an appropriate social networking site specifically designed for under 13's is *What's What*[72] which makes good use of technology by requiring webcam identification and parental approval to ensure that only children can use the site. It has default restrictions on the age range which your child can befriend (normally only one grade above and one below without express

[71]http://www.microsoft.com/security/family-safety/kids-social.aspx
[72]https://www.whatswhat.me/

parental permission on a case by case basis), and also employs professional moderators to keep an eye on things as well as giving parental access to their child's postings – but only to their child's postings. No adults are allowed to use this site at all and the use of web cam identification enforces this.

In general, the social networking concept is about reaching out to make connections with others – either with those who share a common or complementary interest. It is not about collecting large numbers of random 'friends' with whom your child has no real relationship and it is good to encourage your child to distinguish between these types of relationships and to look at shared values and interests in the connections they make on-line.

Pleased to meet you

At informal gatherings with adults and children, the children often run off to play together and leave the adults to get on with it, but you can encourage your child to learn the art of respectful conversation with adults if they are happy to hang around. Try to find opportunities for your child to meet friends of yours, or others within your professional or personal networks.

You could also take your child to meetings where appropriate, particularly if you have to work over the Summer holidays or perhaps as part of a 'take your son/daughter to work day' which will give them opportunities to see and even participate in communication in the workplace.

The Apprentice winner and Chairman of *Bright Ideas Trust, Tim Campbell MBE, has always got his daughter Kayla involved in his work, particularly at weekends and half-terms when there's no school. When he was setting up the Bright Ideas Trust she helped him sort and clean the offices, and when they were running workshops she would sit in on them and contribute.*

Encourage older children to shake hands, to show an interest in what others are saying and adopt good listening skills. Help them to master the art of small talk by role play. Have fun by pretending you are at a function and would like to know more about 'this young man' or 'young woman.' They will learn through practice and will at least know how to respond when at a real function.

Mum of three, Cheryl Ryder, remembers her father introducing her to some of his contacts who then gave her interviews and opportunities to talk through plans before she went to university. She found this incredibly useful.

Phone free zone

Modern technology keeps us connected 24 hours a day, but this constant connectivity can have its problems. Being available 24 hours a day means being tempted to check emails or text messages, 'just in case someone has tried to make contact.' This has resulted in the ability to be 'elsewhere' despite being present. Create a Phone free zone, where your child has your undivided attention. This might mean banning it from the dinner table, so that at least for one meal each day you can talk freely without interruption or furtive glances at your phone. If you feel it's rude for your teen to be texting while you talk to them, then lead by example. You want your child to be an engaging conversationalist when they are older so it is good to model the sort of behaviour you would like your child to adopt: no peeking at your phone while they try to talk to you!

Making new friends

Your child will be mixing with a variety of peer groups within secondary school, so there will be many opportunities for them to make new friends.

However, outside of school, volunteering presents an excellent opportunity to meet new people while getting involved in a worthy cause. Whether through working with new volunteer colleagues, meeting members of the public or attending charitable functions, all are excellent opportunities to network with others.

WHAT YOUR CHILD IS LEARNING

Entrepreneurial networking is about understanding the value that people can bring to the task of taking an enterprise forwards; it provides access to an enlarged 'team' by establishing mutual or reciprocal interests, new alliances and connections.

Good networkers are good collaborators and see the value of working together as a means of attaining a common goal. Encouraging your child to have good conversational skills has an obvious benefit, therefore, as people are naturally drawn to someone who is interesting and engaging.

Give your child opportunities to practise their networking skills within their local community and provide guidance and help in enabling them to make the best and safest use of social networking opportunities.

Giving it back and making their mark

Creating value is one of the defining features of the entrepreneurial way. The assumption is often made that being enterprising is just about making money, but it is of course far wider than that – not only do entrepreneurs bring new products and services to market, they also contribute to the cultural well-being of a society by promoting creativity and individualism whilst creating enterprises that bring people closer together through teamwork and common interests.

The relatively broad term 'value' was chosen to include those individuals referred to as social entrepreneurs: people whose creative drive addresses social needs and solves social problems and who invest all their profits back into this overriding social mission.

No discussion of the entrepreneurial lifestyle, especially as it relates to the upbringing of your child, would be complete without looking at activities explicitly directed at raising their social awareness and ways of harnessing their creative energies for explicitly altruistic purposes.

Building upon the 6-9 years' *Giving it Back* activities, your child can now be introduced to practical examples of how to give back to society and make a positive contribution to the welfare of others. They can learn how it is possible, in spite of their young age, to either have a say in, or even take action on, the things that they care deeply about, through exploring with them in an age appropriate way, local and global social issues, and inspiring in them the desire to do more.

A good starting place is to first look at the particular needs and issues that social enterprise in its broadest sense, exists to address. This can include charities and campaigning groups as well as more business orientated social enterprises.

What would make the world better?

This activity starts with your child writing down what they think are the most important issues that prevent the world being a better and happier place.

Their list might include issues such as cruelty, hunger, disease, poverty, pollution or some more specific examples. If your child is by nature analytical they are most likely to come up with a general classification, which you can then encourage them to fill in examples of. If they have more concrete thinking they will probably make a list of problems that fall under the general headings, for example cruelty to animals, bullying at school, specific diseases, in which case you can then encourage them to try and make sense of the range of issues through clarifying what sort of problem it is.

This is not about having right or wrong answers. Whatever the list of problems they end up with, it is useful at this stage and more likely to help motivate your child to identify in very general terms what would be the opposite to these problems: so world hunger has as its converse a world of plenty with everyone having access to the food and water they needed; the opposite of disease is health and so on. The idea is just to help your child start thinking about the issues, with the assumption that these problems are not intractable and inevitable but could yield to human endeavour with the right ideas, actions and motivation. You could call these converse scenarios opportunities – for that is what they are, there *is* the opportunity to tackle world hunger, many diseases are preventable, we could be kinder and more compassionate, but we have not yet identified the means or had the will. The focus of this activity is to inspire and motivate not to induce despair and apathy.

A caring community

Once your child has a list of problems and opportunities, help them identify which they would most like to explore and research further by identifying appropriate organisations who deal with particular issues. Help them see that each organisation will have a mission statement, take time to discuss the importance of these statements – namely to help each employee or volunteer work together towards a common goal. It also helps the beneficiaries of the organisation understand clearly how they can be helped.

Examples of mission statements are:

Our vision is a world where every cat is treated with kindness and an understanding of its needs. Cats Protection League[73]

We are a different kind of environmental organisation. We focus on people and how they can take practical action in their everyday lives for a better world. Global Action Plan[74]

Shelter believes everyone should have a home. We help people find and keep a home. We campaign for decent housing for all. Shelter[75]

These are well known, non-profit organisations in the U.K. but your child might also like to explore whether there are relevant local, or branches of national, organisations in their community. What can your child learn about them and how do they help the local community, or specific groups within the community?

Help your child to understand the difference between non-profit and profit organisations. Discuss the fact that unlike profit led businesses which share out an element of the profit with the

[73]The Cats Protection League www.cats.org.uk
[74]Global Action Plan www.globalactionplan.org.uk
[75]Shelter http://england.shelter.org.uk and http://scotland.shelter.org.uk

businesses owners, non-profit organisations put any money made back into running the business and the extra income as resources back into the community.

After learning about each mission statement and the work each organisation does, is there one that your child feels particularly drawn to? As a pet lover, it might be an animal welfare organisation, or perhaps for family reasons they might feel an affinity with a particular medical charity, or just feel an altruistic concern prompted by the publicity generated by charities around famine and starving children. This is a good opportunity to delve deeper into their interests, particularly if they are showing signs of wanting to have more of an active role in the community.

My sustainable fridge is 'powered' by dirty water

Young British inventor, *Emily Cummins*, has a passion about sustainable designs that change lives. Among her inventions is the sustainable fridge powered by dirty water which is now used across Southern Africa and improves the quality of both the lives of the women who are creating them and the people who are able to use them. Developing the fridge required a considerable amount of research but as Emily said:

...when I realised I could help people with my products, they became even more important and I wanted them to be the very best they possibly could.

Fundraising

Fundraising is an important part of a non-profit organisation's revenue. If there is an opportunity to involve your child in your own fundraising efforts, talk to them about the charity you are supporting, why it is important to you and why you want to take part. If your fundraising works towards an event such as *Race for Life*, or even a skydive, they will undoubtedly cheer you on during the day itself. Perhaps afterwards, they can help to collect the funds or if you're collecting through charity giving websites, see the total raised and comments made by supporters. Seeing the whole process, from approaching sponsors, the actual event, and afterwards, shows the whole process of giving. Can you take it a step further and introduce your child to the people whom the charity benefits? This will depend on what the charity is and your child's ability to cope with potentially sensitive subjects, but can give them a real sense of achievement.

Volunteering

No charity could function without its volunteers and, once again, this is where your child can have an active part to play. Perhaps there is a local care home for the elderly, who would appreciate someone coming in to read, play the piano, or play a board game. This offers a lovely way to meet mature members of the community who may have interesting tales to tell of when they were young.

Animal welfare charities give your child an opportunity to care for pets; planting trees or caring for gardens are a great way to get outdoors, keep fit, healthy, and be actively involved in something worthwhile at the same time.

There are many opportunities to get involved locally. Research these together and encourage your child to choose one they are particularly interested in.

Do your own thing

What to do if your child has a burning desire to start a project themselves? *GenerationOn*[76] has an excellent downloadable guide, *Do your own thing guide for teens*, which details all the steps they can take, to help them determine:

- What project to tackle?
- Where the need is?
- Who benefits and who can help?
- How to manage the project?

It's an excellent guide, which is easy for your child to understand and provides a handy list of causes to give some ideas to start on.

Beyond charity

Wanting to support charities tackling specific problems is a good and healthy response to the ethical drive to make the world a better place, but there are other possible positive responses which you can explore with your child if they show an interest.

One response may be referred to as the *technocratic* response. Faced with, for example, evidence of suffering caused by disease your child may feel drawn to make a long term goal of pursuing medicine or medical research; or they may feel drawn to finding other technical solutions to one or other of the world's problems, such as *Emily Cummins*, quoted earlier, did.

A further response is a political or campaigning one: your child feels drawn to change what they see as underlying problems such as unequal distribution of wealth or exploitation of human and natural resources. Youthful idealism and zeal for change is a precious commodity and has the power to change things, as events in the Arab Spring have most recently demonstrated, so it's

[76]GenerationOn: www.generationon.org

important to take children's ideas seriously. Sometimes it takes the eyes of a child to see the absurdity of much of what is considered to be sophisticated *realpolitik* – sometimes the Emperor really does have no clothes.

Finally there is the pure social entrepreneurial response: faced with a problem, your child begins to think of sustainable ways that the problem can be tackled without relying upon charitable donations, using some form of business model. This might be as simple as raising money for a cause though selling a product or service, or something more imaginative that somehow ties the business model to the relief of the issue in question. A classic example of this latter approach was the founding of *The Big Issue* as an initiative to help the homeless help themselves, or the development of the micro-loans model in the developing world.[77]

It is perhaps unlikely that your child will arrive overnight at the idea for a new social enterprise as a result of any of the activities in this section, but you will have sown the seeds and if the motivation is there, and you are successful in your efforts to help your child develop their entrepreneurial potential, who knows what the future may hold.

[77]http://www.lendwithcare.org/

WHAT YOUR CHILD IS LEARNING

The activities here will help your child to develop characteristics such as imagination, ambition and visionary thinking. Albert Einstein said, *'We cannot solve the problems that we have created with the same thinking that created them in the first place.'* If ever there was an area in which the creative thinking and drive of the entrepreneur was needed it is in the struggle to address the many challenges that we are presented with to make our world a better, more sustainable, kinder and fairer place.

By encouraging your child to be actively involved in the work of non-profit organisations, you help them to see the different methods that organisations use to address the big social issues around us. By introducing them to business concepts and methods, and developing their potential entrepreneurial characteristics, you are also giving your child a set of tools that they can apply to the problems they see in the world and use to transform problems into opportunities and to realise real social value.

Interview with Tim Campbell MBE, *The Apprentice* winner and founder of *Bright Ideas Trust*

TIM CAMPBELL MBE had a successful career with London Underground until being thrust into the public eye by participating in and winning the British version of the hit TV series *The Apprentice* in 2005. After spending two years with Sir Alan Sugar at *Amstrad*, he left to establish *Bright Ideas Trust* – a nationwide social enterprise charity which encourages and supports young people aged 16 to 25 from disadvantaged backgrounds to start business ventures.

Now Chairman, Tim splits his time between continuing to support the Trust he founded and his other roles as the Mayor of London's Ambassador for Training and Enterprise, a government business advisor[78], and speaking engagements. In 2012 Tim received a MBE in the Queen's 2012 New Year Honours list for his services to enterprise culture.

Tim is 34 years old and lives in East London with his wife Jasmine and their two children Kayla aged 11 and Aaron aged 2.

---

[78]http://www.businesszone.co.uk/topic/business-trends/breaking-news-big-name-entrepreneurs-join-new-government-advisory-forum/31700

TELL US A LITTLE ABOUT YOUR CHILDHOOD, FAMILY VALUES, AND YOUR MOTHER'S INFLUENCE ON YOUR LIFE

I'm the oldest of three children brought up by my single mum. She held down three jobs to make ends meet, working in the rag trade in Whitechapel, cleaning offices, then coming home and using her seamstress skills to make clothes and curtains, as well as baking and selling amazing cakes. What I remember most of all was how incredibly hard she worked. She didn't call herself an 'entrepreneur' but that's what she was.'

Tim goes on to explain how that work ethic of taking responsibility for making ends meet rather than relying on handouts or benefits, had a major influence on him.

I'm a normal person,' he says 'not ultra-clever, I just know the power of working really hard and what that can achieve. People often get hung up on talents and innate abilities but the reality is if you don't work hard then you're wasting your time.'

WERE THERE TIMES AS A CHILD WHEN YOU WONDERED WHY YOUR MUM WORKED SO HARD?

'Absolutely', replies Tim without hesitation, *'As a young child I remember Mum working all night, often in tears, struggling to keep things going. I didn't like the fact that she worked such long hours. There were often times when I would ask her "why can't you just go to bed?" It's only now that I realise just what she put herself through to support us all. Sometimes she would get us involved in helping her make belt loops for hundreds of trousers, which then meant she could get to bed a little earlier. Of course we didn't understand that at the time, we just enjoyed playing the game she made up for us. I guess you could say back then that ignorance really was bliss.'*

Tim talks about how his mother instilled good manners in her children *'using some of her famous Jamaican discipline to keep us in line,'* he laughs, and mentions the effort she made to ensure the financial difficulties at home were not evident to the outside world, with the children being well turned out with tidy clothes and polished shoes. Tim clearly knew as a child that they didn't have as much as others, but to the outside world they were just like any other family.

WHAT KIND OF ACTIVITIES DID YOU ENJOY DOING AS A CHILD?
'I wasn't really a team player when it came to sports, preferring running or martial arts to the more traditional team sports of football or rugby. I also loved to read. I remember every Friday we would have a fish and chips tea and provided I completed my chores well, Mum would buy the Beano *or* Dandy *comic. I'd wolf down my food so I could start reading the comic as quickly as possible.'*

Tim smiles remembering how every week his mum used to tell him not to read the comic all at once as it had to last him until the following week, but of course by the end of the weekend he had read it cover to cover.

WHAT WAS YOUR MOTHER'S ATTITUDE TO YOUR EDUCATION?
'Mum was obsessed about all of us doing well and completing our education. She wanted us to try our very best at school and if I came home with a 'C' grade she wanted to know why it wasn't a 'B', or if it was a 'B' why it wasn't an 'A'. She encouraged and pushed us to see what we could achieve – to realise our potential.'

Tim goes on to describe his mum as a *'brilliant coach'* and how although some might view her approach as pushy, her ambitions for all the children were grounded in the reality of the potential she saw in each of them.

SO WHAT WAS SCHOOL LIKE FOR YOU?
'Primary school was fine, but by the time I reached secondary I started to understand more clearly with a far wider community of children

the fact that I didn't have as much as others did. I think it was also at that point that I realised why Mum had to earn more than anyone-else just to make sure we had the basics.'

It was at secondary school, however, that Tim started to get in to trouble, often playing truant. *'I wasn't in a good place and I didn't feel there was an adult I could talk to about the struggles I was having, trying to understand who I was, and what my place was in the world. The testosterone was starting to fly and I could so easily have taken a different path at that point,'* he reflects.

Fortunately for Tim there was one teacher, an Irish man named Mr Gerry Foley[79], who, in Tim's words, *'saved me. Mr Foley was a cool teacher; he was young and inspired in me a thirst for knowledge and taught me to question assumptions. He opened my eyes to how important it is to question the status quo and taught me that I could control my own destiny with focus and determination.'*

Through this difficult time, Tim's mum never gave up on him either. She would meet with the teachers and tell them that she would provide whatever help they needed to keep Tim in education, even if that meant sitting in the class with him every day.

Tim describes Mr Foley as his *'very first mentor'* and after appearing on *The Apprentice*, he decided to track Mr Foley down and they now stay in regular contact.

Tim's greatest aspiration at that time was to get through school, and with the support of Mr Foley as well as his mum, he did just that and went on to study at university.

SO WHAT HAPPENED AT AND AFTER UNIVERSITY?

'Well, the timing was right to go to university,' says Tim. *'I needed to be independent from the family home and only through that distance could I then really understand and appreciate the sacrifices Mum had made for all of us.'*

[79]http://www.belvederecollege.ie/welcome.html

Being the first to go to university (Tim graduated from Middlesex University with a 2:1 in Psychology) his mother was naturally very proud of him, *'sending everyone in Jamaica my certificate.'*

'As far as Mum was concerned, she'd done her job,' Tim reflects, however although he found the university experience helpful in his pursuit of learning as well as providing opportunities for reflection, Tim didn't have any strong passion or desire to be there. *'I left university not really knowing what to do next. I had no clear guidance on what to do with my degree apart from remembering what Mum had said that once I've earned it then it can't be taken away'.*

SO DID HE TALK WITH HIS MOTHER ABOUT THIS?
'No, I couldn't do that,' he quickly responds. *'I saw how much joy my achievement gave her and didn't want to take that away,'* so he chose to speak with his two closest friends, Jasmine (now his wife) and Paul, and they helped him work through the possibilities and direction to take.

'I think I realised that I was much more suited to being out and about and talking with people than anything else,' says Tim. *'I'm a good salesman and I seem to have inherited that West Indian chameleon-like ability to adapt to situations.'* he laughs.

LOOKING AT YOUR OWN CHILDREN NOW (KAYLA, 11 AND AARON, 2),
HOW DO YOU BELIEVE YOU ARE INFLUENCING THEM WITH REGARD TO
DEVELOPING THEIR ENTREPRENEURIAL POTENTIAL?
'Jasmine and I are passionate about ensuring we don't bring up children who are spoilt. Kayla has seen us both working so understands that much of what we have, such as a nice house, cars and so on, are achieved by working really hard, there's no shortcut. My heart sank the other day when we went into a well-known department store to discover that Monopoly now has a credit card included in the game, I mean what's that teaching children?'

'We teach Kayla basic manners so she grows up respecting both

herself and others, and of course that relationships should be equal, but we also teach her that she has the right to go and achieve whatever she wants.'

Tim has always got Kayla involved in his work, particularly at weekends and half-terms when there's no school. When he was setting up the Bright Ideas Trust she helped him sort and clean the offices, and when they were running workshops she would sit in on them and contribute.

'I think her horizons of considering what is possible are significantly broader than mine were at that age,' reflects Tim, *'and I can see how the way in which we influence her is manifesting itself. At just 11 years old, Kayla is very focused on "well why can't I make something to sell or do something to get the money for what I want" rather than just saying "I want that."*

'Our greatest duty is and has been to make sure Kayla believes anything is possible. We don't lie to her that achievement is easy, she knows you have to put in a lot of hard work, but I can see that mindset developing in her, see her thinking about how she is going to make something happen. Yes, there is a basic level of education we believe she should receive, that's not negotiable, but after that then if she has a reasonable plan for something then we'll support her'.

Tim talks about how when he and Jasmine were helping Kayla prepare for her 11 plus exam (in which she did really well), they emphasised to her and made it clear that she didn't have to do it, that she could pull out at any time. *'To our amazement,'* he continues, *'she actually wrote a proposal telling us all the reasons why she should be taking it, so there was no doubt in our minds that she was doing it for herself rather than for us.'*

'We're going through a big debate at home at the moment,' Tim mentions, *'about at what age Kayla should have a mobile phone of her own. I'm not sure she should have one yet, so she wrote me a note*

telling me why she should have one. It was hard to disagree with her reasoned logic!'

Tim and Jasmine incentivise Kayla to do well: *'If she gets good results at school then she knows she will be able to choose where she wants to go, such as having dinner, or the theatre. It works well, although I have been forced to sit through the odd musical which has sometimes been painful,'* he reflects. *'Actually I think we owe her a treat at the moment.*

'First and most importantly, make whatever you do fun! Fun isn't talked about in business, but it should be and activities at home should be full of fun and engaging for children.

Secondly, remember that as a parent you can't set the agenda. Let your child take the lead in an activity otherwise you may actually lose some really powerful learning, and avoid being too prescriptive about how to do things. Kayla does martial arts and I encourage her to show Aaron what she does, so she is learning presentation skills, and she's also teaching me too. Giving your child responsibility and choices is crucial for their confidence and learning; just be careful not to overload them and above all make sure they are enjoying themselves.

Thirdly, I'd say help your child get as many new experiences as possible, these don't have to cost money, it could be simply visiting the library, a museum, or going for a walk in the park. Take time to think about what you're doing in a child-like way and see the wonder of the everyday. We are touched by enterprise wherever we go; it's not difficult to find inspiration from everyday things if you look through children's eyes.

Finally, remember that as parents we can't be expected to know all the answers, it's just not possible. Use and leverage your own networks to fill in the gaps.'

You can read more about Tim's business activities and his work at Bright Ideas Trust by visiting **www.brightideastrust.com**

Enterprising employees of the future

I think people forget that 98% of businesses in this country are small and medium enterprises... The vast majority are entrepreneurial in nature. Giving children a basic understanding of these skills would undoubtedly equip them better for the workplace.

Nicola Horlick, business leader and entrepreneur

There is no shortage of reports detailing the fact that employers feel young people are lacking crucial skills and attitudes when they come to join the workplace. An analysis of these reports shows clear evidence of a crossover between what are being defined as *employability* skills and what is being focused on here in terms of *entrepreneurial* characteristics.

Entrepreneurial skills and attitudes are not just essential for young people thinking about starting their own business, but in an era of unprecedented high youth unemployment (forecast to rise globally to 12.7% of 15-24 year olds this year, equating to nearly 75 million young people[80]), those who begin to realise their entrepreneurial potential will stand out and have the advantage over others as employers seek new recruits with key skills, such as a solution focused approach to problems, strong team working abilities, commercial awareness, and excellent communication and interpersonal skills.

In 2007, a publication[81] by the *Confederation of British Industry*

[80]http://apprenticeshipblog.com/2012/05/22/global-youth-unemployment-rate-predicted-12-7-until-2016/
[81]'Time well spent: Embedding employability in work experience' report, March 2007

(CBI), the United Kingdom's leading business organisation representing some 240,000 businesses that together employ around a third of the private sector workforce, examined the range of skills employers were looking for and whether young recruits were meeting these requirements.

These *employability* skills were defined by the CBI as

> *... a set of attributes, skills and knowledge that all labour market participants should possess to ensure they have the capability of being effective in the workplace – to the benefit of themselves, their employer and the wider economy.*

and are detailed below:

Exhibit 31 **CBI definition of employability skills**
A positive attitude (readiness to take part, openness to new ideas and activities, desire to achieve) underpinning:

Self-management – readiness to accept responsibility, flexibility, time management, readiness to improve own performance

Teamworking – respecting others, co-operating, negotiating/persuading, contributing to discussions

Business and customer awareness – basic understanding of the key drivers for business success and the need to provide customer satisfaction

Problem solving – analysing facts and circumstances and applying creative thinking to develop appropriate solutions

Communication and literacy – application of literacy, ability to produce clear, structured written work and oral literacy, including listening and questioning

Application of numeracy – manipulation of numbers, general mathematical awareness and its application in practical contexts

Application of information technology – basic IT skills, including familiarity with word processing, spreadsheets, file management and use of internet search engines

---

© Confederation of British Industry, *reproduced with kind permission*

It is evident both from this report and the subsequent one in 2011[82] that there is still a considerable way to go before the gap is narrowed between the skills and attitudes employers require and what new young recruits are able to offer.

Charlie Mayfield, Chairman of Britain's most successful and well-known employee-owned company, *John Lewis Partnership,* believes that:

> *Only by providing young people with a wide range of skills – both formal and behavioural – are we going to fully equip them for the workplace, drive enterprise and create economic growth.*

The range of skills Mr Mayfield refers to are those detailed in a report in 2009[83] by the *UK Commission for Employment and Skills (UK Commission)*, of which he is currently Chairman. The *Employability Challenge* report outlines employability skills as being '...*critical to economic competitiveness and to the ability of individuals to get and progress in rewarding work.'* An employer-led organisation, 'with Commissioners drawn from the highest levels of private, public, and voluntary sectors, supported by trade union leadership,' it has incorporated in its study views from 200 organisations including schools, colleges, private and public sector employers.

The *UK Commission* outlines its own definition of employability skills as built on a *'Positive Approach'* foundation – new recruits being ready to participate, make suggestions, accept new ideas and constructive criticism, and take responsibility for outcomes. This foundation supports a number of *Functional Skills,* focusing on numeracy, literacy, and information technology, which are exercised in the context of *Personal Skills:*

[82] 'Building for growth: business priorities for education and skills', CBI/EDI Education and Skills survey 2011
[83] The Employability Challenge, UK Commission, February 2009

- *Self management* – punctuality and time management, fitting dress and behaviour to context, overcoming challenges and asking for help when necessary.
- *Thinking and solving problems* – creativity, reflecting on and learning from own actions, prioritising, analysing situations, and developing solutions.
- *Working together and communicating* – co-operating, being assertive, persuading, being responsible to others, speaking clearly to individuals and groups and listening for a response.
- *Understanding the business* – understanding how the individual job fits into the organisation as a whole; recognising the needs of stakeholders (customers and service users, for example); judging risks, innovating, and contributing to the whole organisation.

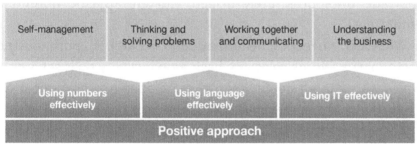

© UK Commission for Employment and Skills reproduced with kind permission

In the same year, *Young Enterprise*[84], the United Kingdom's largest business and enterprise education charity, commissioned a survey[85] of the 28 *'most important and influential companies in the UK'* who between them have 715,000 employees and members, asking among other things what skills, if any, are young people currently missing when they present themselves as potential recruits. Of particular interest were the results that:

[84]www.young-enterprise.org.uk
[85]Business Education Survey 2011, Freshminds poll of 28 top UK companies for Young Enterprise

- 59% felt that the education system was poor at developing young people's entrepreneurial skills, and
- Approximately 75% felt that the British education system is not equipping young people with the right skills for them to enter the workforce.

When asked to detail specific skills the companies felt young people were missing, the replies included business acumen, entrepreneurial skills, economic context, business awareness, commercial acumen, emotional intelligence, leadership, personal learning and thinking skills, finance/enterprise, and communication skills.

In whichever way *employability* skills are defined – The *UK Commission* research uncovered 20 typical ones, there can be no doubt that the current education system is not addressing the shortage of appropriately skilled and enthusiastic potential employees.

Whilst certain requirements may differ depending upon industry sector or specific job roles, the basic employability skills set is one which will, without doubt, enable young people to be in a better position to compete for available jobs.

The key areas which define employability skills, such as self-management, an ability to work in a team, problem solving, communication, and commercial awareness, are all addressed through the activities in this book, covering the five entrepreneurial characteristics of *Perception of Possibilities, Ambition, Risk and Resolve, Teamwork*, and *Value*.

Paul Lindley, founder of Ella's Kitchen, which turns over around £60 million pounds worth of global retail sales, said in his interview earlier in this book that he believes the mindset of prospective employees is equally as important as the skills themselves.

The opportunities for parents to help develop a child's entrepreneurial potential from an early age are immense and, whilst many employers would not necessarily expect their new young recruits to excel at everything, they are almost certainly more likely to invest in continuing training and education for those who show potential[86].

The marketplace may be global, but globalisation means the world is becoming smaller, making it an increasingly competitive environment within which to trade. This competition also extends to the recruitment of staff, where geographical boundaries are no longer an issue for many employers so the recruitment pool is significantly larger now than previously.

As parents, we may not be able to do much about the macroeconomic factors affecting our children's future, but we *can* help to nurture in them the attitudes and skills they will need to become active participants rather than bystanders in the unfolding of the future, and that is surely the least that we owe to them, whether they go on to become business owners, leaders, or actively engaged employees.

---

[86]Links to new reports due out July 2012 from the UK Commission regarding structural changes in the youth labour market and an employers' guide to recruiting young people are available on the Enterprising Child web site.

Interview with Nicola Horlick,
business leader and entrepreneur

 **NICOLA HORLICK** is a business leader and entrepreneur who has founded and led highly successful businesses while juggling the demands of raising a family.

She joined S.G. *Warburg* as a graduate trainee in 1983 and helped to create *Mercury Asset Management*, where she was appointed a director at only 28 years old.

In 1991 Nicola moved to *Morgan Grenfell Asset Management* where in 1992, she was appointed Managing Director of Morgan Grenfell's UK business. Over the following five years, funds under management increased from £4 billion to £22 billion. *Morgan Grenfell* became recognised as one of the leading managers of UK pension funds.

In 1997, Nicola went on to set up *SG Asset Management* for the French bank *Société Générale* and subsequently founded *Bramdean Asset Management* in 2005. In more recent years, she has focused her efforts on developing film projects through her company *Derby Street Films* and has opened a restaurant in Barnes called *Georgina's.* She is also Chairman of a new investment company called *Rockpool*.

Nicola is the mother of six children – Georgina, Alice, Serena, Antonia, Rupert and Benjie. Her eldest daughter Georgina tragically died of leukaemia in 1998 at the age of 12.

DO YOU THINK SCHOOLS ARE SUFFICIENTLY EQUIPPING YOUNGSTERS WITH THE SKILLS THEY NEED TO ENTER THE WORKPLACE?

I think it largely depends upon the school. There are very good schools which bring practical, entrepreneurial type projects into the classroom – I personally have been involved in judging entrepreneurial competitions in some of these schools. However, I do think more practical skills could be brought into the curriculum: for example, teaching children how to manage money, how to save, how to write a CV, or even how to write a business plan. I think people forget that 98% of businesses in this country are small and medium enterprises. Only 2% are multi-national businesses like Glaxo. The vast majority are entrepreneurial in nature. Giving children a basic understanding of these skills would undoubtedly equip them better for the workplace.

WHEN WE TAKE SKILLS SUCH AS CUSTOMER SERVICE, COMMERCIAL AWARENESS, TEAMWORK AND RESILIENCE, DO YOU THINK YOUNGSTERS HAVE THESE SUFFICIENTLY? WHAT DO YOU THINK CAN BE DONE TO HELP YOUNGSTERS BE BETTER EQUIPPED WITH THESE SKILLS?

Anyone who lacks experience will need to be trained in order to perform a job well. Young people going into the workplace are unlikely to have commercial awareness if it is their first job. However, they should have some idea of how to work in a team environment as many subjects at school are now taught in a way which involves collaboration, and team sports obviously encourage that too. Resilience is a characteristic that some will have and some will not. Customer service will come naturally to some and will need to be instilled in others.

**HOW HAVE YOU INFLUENCED YOUR OWN CHILDREN — ARE THEY
SHOWING SIGNS OF ENTREPRENEURIAL POTENTIAL?**

*My son was very entrepreneurial from an early age. When he was 14,
he bought rugs and a consignment of footballs and sold them on at a
profit, which was very amusing. My daughter Alice has set up her own
handbag business. She is working on her first collection now and is
travelling to Italy shortly to oversee the cutting out of the leather at
the factory that she is using. She's a good all-rounder, but very
creative — an incredibly talented portraitist. She did a portrait of her
younger brother and it almost looks like a photograph.*

*I did not sit them down and teach them to be entrepreneurial,
although undoubtedly they have seen me busy working over the
years.*

**HOW WOULD YOU SAY YOUR PARENTS INFLUENCED YOUR OWN
WORK ETHIC, AND WHAT TIPS DO YOU HAVE FOR OTHER PARENTS
WHO ARE KEEN TO ENCOURAGE THEIR CHILD'S POTENTIAL?**

*My father ran a company which my grandfather set up. He made it
an extremely successful business. I worked there between 1982 and
1983 and my father really encouraged me and believed in me. I think
girls in particular can be self-doubting. My daughter Alice has a lot of
self-belief and is incredibly confident, but my other daughters need
to be encouraged quite a bit. I grew up surrounded by boys, so didn't
feel at all intimidated in a workplace which was predominantly male,
which is where I think fathers in particular can help a great deal. I
think my advice would be simply to encourage your child to have a go
and to not give up.*

Interviews with young entrepreneurs

Tim Armoo

Louis Barnett

Adam Bradford

Luke Cousins

Emily Cummins

Jamie Dunn

James Headspeath

Jennifer Okpapi

TIMOTHY ARMOO is a 17 year old, young entrepreneur from South London and founder of *EntrepreneurXpress*, the first UK magazine aimed at inspiring young people and equipping them with the know-how and skills to become involved in entrepreneurship.

Before this, Timothy founded and ran an events management business, organising parties and raves. His first company, a tutoring business, was founded at the age of 14 based on a bet that he would not make £500 before he was 18. By the time the company had wound up, he had made twice that amount within three months, reaching a peak of 65 tutors.

TELL US A LITTLE ABOUT YOUR BACKGROUND, AND HOW YOU FEEL YOUR PARENTS NURTURED YOUR ENTREPRENEURIAL POTENTIAL.

I wouldn't say that my parents necessarily instilled the idea of me becoming an entrepreneur. However, both parents were hard-working, especially my dad.

From a young age, I saw him working incredibly hard. I think this made me decide that I didn't want to become an employee. He definitely showed me the value of hard work, how to run the whole show, as it were. He certainly wanted to ensure that I studied well.

One thing he always used to say to me was 'hard work won't kill you, but laziness will!' I never understood it at the time, but now, I see what he means. We're designed to be active. I much prefer to be on the go. He also taught me not to settle for second best, and that's a valuable lesson for me nowadays.

DO YOU HAVE ANY ADVICE FOR OTHER YOUNGSTERS, WHO MIGHT BE CONSIDERING ENTREPRENEURSHIP?

I would say just do it – although I would say it's important to speak to other people about going into business. You need a mentor – I have many mentors. But you also need the emotional support of your parents – I couldn't have coped with my events company if I didn't have my mother's shoulder to cry on. There were many challenges with that particular company, and Mum was great for bolstering my confidence to keep going.

Being young is the best time to try these new experiences. You see things from an exciting perspective. You're not afraid to push the boundaries. In a sense, you don't think about what you can't do – you just do it. So I would say use your youth as an opportunity to embrace these wonderful challenges. You are still at home with your parents, you'll have their support and backing, so you've nothing to lose. I like the idea of not being part of the crowd. I hate the humdrum of being 'normal'. I love to be able to continually push myself. So that would be my other piece of advice – stretch yourself.

I think it's also important to embrace technology. The internet has changed the way we are able to work, so use it to your full advantage.

WHAT ADVICE DO YOU HAVE FOR PARENTS, WHO ARE KEEN TO NURTURE THE ENTREPRENEURIAL POTENTIAL IN THEIR CHILDREN?
Encourage your child to try different things. Fraser Doherty's grandmother showed him how to make jam when he was 14 years old. It sparked in him an interest to take it further. He went on to create Super Jam and it's now packed on the shelves of most major supermarkets. So even a simple thing like that can spark an idea in your child, and you never know where it will take you.

Instill in your child that there is no such thing as failure. Lots of kids worry too much about what others might think of them. 'What if my friends laugh at me?' Encourage them to just try it anyway. They have nothing to lose. When I first went to school, I hated rugby, but my parents encouraged me to keep it up. Now I love rugby.

LOUIS BARNETT is a 20 year old entrepreneur, chocolatier and conservationist with a passion for producing products of the highest quality. His business, *Chokolit*, is a growing global enterprise, started when he was just 12 years old. Within three years Louis became the youngest ever supplier to *Waitrose, Sainsbury's*, and *Selfridges*.

Louis was diagnosed with dyslexia, dyspraxia, dyscalculia, and short term memory loss at 11 years of age.

CAN YOU TELL ME A LITTLE ABOUT YOUR CHILDHOOD AND UPBRINGING?

Much the same as the next person I think, although I only have mine as a reference. A loving family who have worked and fought hard for what we've achieved. Very close knit and supportive and for as long as I remember, I've been brought up to strive for what I want to achieve and have always had the backing of my nearest and dearest.

I am severely dyslexic and dyspraxic and this shows up in various ways. I find it incredibly easy to talk about something and I am not fazed by public speaking at all. On the other hand, writing down what I say or think is an impossible task. For a start my handwriting is illegible and I cannot type as fast as I can speak. My mum is also dyslexic but her dyslexia is different from mine: whereas she would be freaked out by having to stand up in front of a room full of people to explain or recount something, in a face-to-face situation or on the phone she can describe things in great detail and is even quite funny. What a team of dyslexics – we always find a way!

WHAT DID YOUR PARENTS DO FOR A LIVING?

My father is still an occupational analyst and my mother used to paint murals and decorate furniture for client's homes. She would love to still have the time to pick up a paintbrush, but with the business expanding so quickly, sadly there doesn't seem to be any spare time!

WHAT DO YOU FEEL YOUR PARENTS' WORK ETHIC IS/WAS AND WHEN DID YOU FIRST BECOME AWARE OF THIS?

I've always been brought up on a very simple set of ethics...Do what you say you are going to do; do it the best you can do it, for as long as it takes. The key is to always follow things through and don't let people down. I can't say when I first became aware of how my parents influenced me; it's always been that way and always will be.

DID YOU HAVE ANY PARTICULAR AMBITIONS AS A CHILD?

I was always very driven as a child; I had an unquenchable thirst for learning and everything had to be explained right from an early age. How something was made, why things were the way they were. I would absorb all this information and then regurgitate it to anyone who was willing to listen.

CAN YOU TELL ME A LITTLE ABOUT WHEN YOU WERE DIAGNOSED WITH DYSLEXIA, DYSPRAXIA, DYSCALCULIA, AND SHORT TERM MEMORY LOSS? HOW DID YOUR PARENTS SUPPORT YOU? WAS THIS THE PROMPT FOR THEM TO TAKE YOU OUT OF MAINSTREAM EDUCATION AND PROVIDE HOME SCHOOLING?

I was diagnosed at the age of 11 and struggled with mainstream education and experienced bullying. Home schooling was a necessity, however it was the best thing that could have happened, because my parents (who were and still are my backbone and incredibly supportive) could provide me with the level of teaching that I craved.

DID YOU EVER FEEL THAT BECAUSE OF ALL THE DIAGNOSES YOU WOULDN'T BE ABLE TO ACHIEVE YOUR AMBITIONS? IF SO, HOW DID YOU OVERCOME THAT FEELING?

I've always had ambition and that didn't change simply because my condition had been given a name. I don't see them as a disadvantage, more of an ability – it's what makes me who I am. With the family work ethic and my thirst for knowledge, I always knew that regardless of success or failure, as long as I worked hard towards my goals, that was the important thing.

DO YOU FEEL THE HOME SCHOOLING YOU RECEIVED ENCOURAGED YOU TO BE MORE ENTERPRISING THAN IF YOU WERE IN MAINSTREAM EDUCATION, AND IF SO IN WHAT WAY?

There's a certain amount of curriculum that you have to follow, guidelines to work around. However, because I was so hungry for information and a very quick learner, being home-schooled meant I could work at a pace set for my abilities and talents.

IN WHICH WAYS DO YOU FEEL YOUR PARENTS INFLUENCED DECISIONS ABOUT STARTING YOUR BUSINESS AT SUCH A YOUNG AGE AND HOW DID THEY SUPPORT YOU?

My parents have never really influenced my decisions; they have supported my ideas and have provided a constant source of encouragement. Both my parents never tried to influence me into choosing a career and just allowed me to find my passion. When I left school for home tutoring they gave me the time to settle into a routine of my own, what best suited me. With time finally all my own I began to look within, what it was I loved doing. One of my passions was working with animals; when I said to my parents that I wanted to experience working with birds of prey my mother found a local falconry centre and booked me a day's course working with them. They encouraged me to volunteer some of my time to work at the centre. When I then announced that I wanted an owl of my own they supported me in achieving this goal too. When finally I realised that I wanted to become a chocolatier and told my parents, they both said they would support me in whatever career I chose as long as it was what made me happy. They both then set about buying small amounts of equipment so I would have the tools to begin working with chocolate. My father helped me research chocolate suppliers and this led to him booking a three day training course at the chocolate Callebaut academy in Banbury, Oxford. They both gave up their time to join in and learn too. My parents are involved with my business and have given me the opportunity to experience all the wonderful things I have achieved.

CAN YOU TELL ME YOUR VIEWS ON WHAT YOU BELIEVE ARE THE MOST IMPORTANT THINGS FOR A YOUNG PERSON TO LEARN TO HELP THEM BECOME MORE 'ENTERPRISING' AND IN PARTICULAR FOR ANY YOUNG PERSON HAVING TO COPE WITH A SIMILAR DIAGNOSIS AND/OR CHALLENGING ISSUES IN THEIR LIVES?
Generally it feels like children aren't allowed to think for themselves any more. Everything is monitored; guidelines are in place to see how well your child is developing and if you don't meet those expectations then you are seen as different. Everyone has the same 24 hours in a day, what you choose to do with them is completely up to you.

WHAT ONE PIECE OF ADVICE WOULD YOU GIVE TO PARENTS READING THIS BOOK WHO WANT TO SUPPORT AND DEVELOP ENTREPRENEURIAL POTENTIAL IN THEIR CHILDREN?
Believe in your child first and foremost, no matter what their dreams are and allow them to go after it and support them in their journey. Completely remove yourself from the equation; it's not about what you want; it's their life and mistakes or successes, the only way to learn is to let them live it.

Be supportive, encouraging and guiding and you will learn along the way too.

You can read more about Louis' story, how he discovered his passion and talent for chocolate, and learn more about his Chokolit brand at www.chokolit.co.uk

ADAM BRADFORD is Director of *UnITe Computing*, a part of *Adam Bradford Enterprise and Investments*. He is a National Ambassador for the Peter Jones' (*Dragons' Den*) Enterprise Academy, and has recently launched '*The Initiative*' supporting young people from disadvantaged backgrounds who want to start a business.

Adam is 19 years old and has Aspergers.

TELL US ABOUT YOUR CHILDHOOD AND WHAT YOUR RELATIONSHIP WITH YOUR PARENTS WAS LIKE

'*I was born premature, nine weeks early, and had what I guess could be called a fairly average childhood*'. Perhaps less 'average' was the fact that by the age of three, Adam could recite the alphabet and talk in coherent, often complex sentences. '*I was considered bright for my age, and this was recognised at both nursery and infant schools,*' says Adam.

His mother was an office administrator, but gave that up to look after him when he was born. '*Dad was, and still is, an accountant,*' explains Adam. '*He occasionally used to get me involved in his work when I was about six or seven, just taking me over to his office so I could mess about on the computer.*' Adam's dad worked locally so they were able to do lots of things together such as enjoying family meal times which were important to them. His parents' work ethic was very much about getting nothing for free and working hard. '*Their attitude was don't rely on other people, if you want something done, do it yourself, accept and be empowered by taking responsibility.*'

'*I had a very close relationship with both my parents,*' Adam continues, '*but when I was four, my twin brothers were born and I guess there were less opportunities for me to interact with my parents so I quickly learned to become independent, although I think Mum would say I tried to rule my own life a little too much! I always wanted to progress, to be in the driving seat, and had a desire to lead, even at that young age.'*

Adam goes on to talk about the change from primary to junior school which had quite a big impact on him. *'I remember that transition from having a huge amount of freedom to be creative when I was in infants to suddenly being in a more structured and can I say boring junior class.'*

It was at that point Adam decided he was wanted to do something different, something more than was being offered in the class, longing for the freedom to be creative and progress. This desire for change and progression caused conflict and some falling out with some of his friends at school, not to mention challenges for the teachers rooted to the mainstream way of doing things.

'I also remember one day a visitor to the school asking me to write down everything that was going round in my head,' said Adam. *'I didn't know at the time, but I think that visitor was an Educational Psychologist who identified that I might have characteristics associated with an Autistic Spectrum Disorder.'*

WAS THIS THE POINT AT WHICH ASPERGERS WAS DIAGNOSED?
'Not really,' explains Adam. *'Aspergers wasn't on the radar as such back then and although my parents spoke with the school about some of the difficulties I was having, the school didn't really know how to respond and felt I was just wasting their time with my constant drive for achievement.'*

However, given the psychologist assessment earlier, and prompted by the long waiting times on the NHS, Adam's parents fast tracked him just at the end of primary school to have a private psychological assessment where Aspergers was confirmed.

By the time he reached secondary school, Adam was really struggling with the fact that his desire to achieve more was not responded to. *'Students struggling to achieve grades were given extra support, but because I wasn't in that category, there was nothing for me. The new school was tough with lots of problems, so I was just viewed as yet another problem, meaning the challenge then lay with me to do the very best I could.'*

Adam explained that although his parents knew it wasn't a particularly good school, they were concerned about continuity and at least staying where he was meant he would be around familiar faces from the previous junior school.

WHAT HAPPENED AFTER THE DIAGNOSIS?

'My parents were very supportive' says Adam, *'and were in regular contact with the school. Some of the teachers did what they could to help, for example I was allowed to take some exams much earlier than normal, but this wasn't really addressing my desire to achieve more.'* By the time Adam was studying for his GCSEs, he ended up going through what he could only describe as *'the worst stresses of the traditional education system you could imagine,'* resulting in his parents taking the difficult decision to move him to a different school to enable him to complete his studies. There's no doubt, hearing Adam tell his story, that this was an incredibly emotional and stressful time for both him and his family, yet he managed do well in his exams (*'the new school was really good, supporting and believing in me'*) achieving 27 A*-C GCSEs.

The whole experience of what happened at the other school, though, took its toll on both him and his family. *'It just felt like we'd been broken down,'* says Adam., *'We all needed time to recover from what had happened and it was like we were treading water to keep going, but without the usual smiley, positive approach to life I'd become used to in the family.'*

SO HOW DID YOU END UP AT THE PETER JONES ENTERPRISE ACADEMY AND RUNNING YOUR OWN BUSINESS?

'When I was 14 there was a business competition run through the school. We basically had £25 to invest in a business idea. I worked with class friends to develop a series of resources for the interactive whiteboards at school to help teachers learn how to use them. We won £10,000 worth of prizes which was fantastic and my first venture in to entrepreneurial activity.'

After everything he'd been through though, Adam needed time to recover and put ideas of business to one side. It was during this recovery period, however, that he came across the Peter Jones Enterprise Academy (PJEA) and wanted to find out more. *'My interest in business was sparked after realising how much I enjoyed entering and winning the competition at school and I was keen to follow that route,'* says Adam. His parents were less convinced and probably would have preferred him to follow a more traditional route such as going to university, but it was a meeting with a careers adviser which swung it. *'She told me that after everything I'd been through I shouldn't worry about whether I'm getting top grades, whether my work is the best or even right, I should just do what makes me happy. It was one of the best pieces of advice I've ever received.'*

Adam applied to, and was successful in being accepted to the PJEA. *'It was a really practical course and very intense, huge amounts of work but I felt able to cope, I loved it, it just ignited my passion for business,'* he says. During the course Adam decided to start his own business, Unite computing: an IT solutions, training and consultancy company. Since leaving PJEA he has grown and expanded the company to include the Adam Bradford Enterprise and Investments Group and is now mentored by successful 'Reggae Reggae' sauce entrepreneur and *Dragons' Den* survivor, Levi Roots.

'*They've been great,*' says Adam, '*really supportive and they've helped me to see many of the similarities between running a business and bringing up a child. For example to me it's like I have become a parent to my business and we've talked a lot together about those parallels. The first five years are all about taking small steps, structuring the day, being creative, exploring new places (opportunities) and actually applying general common sense to everyday tasks.*'

Adam has a very strict view about not borrowing money to finance his business ventures and believes in part this is influenced by his dad. '*Running a business isn't for everyone,*' says Adam, '*and one of the best ways to know if you're suited to it is if you really can make something out of nothing – starting with a zero balance and building from there.*' Adam feels his parents' instincts are usually spot on and have encouraged him to do what they felt he could achieve: '*They know me better than I know myself,*' he says and goes on to describe how he always uses his '*mother's touch*' first in business, that 'gut instinct' as to how he feels about things. '*My mum is probably one of the most un-entrepreneurial people I know,*' he laughs '*yet her touch is what works for me in business. I often wonder what she'd be like running a business but she is quite traditional and probably wouldn't like the lack of security and amount of risk.*'

His dad, on the other hand, influences the more strategic approach to the business. '*Dad comes in to play after I've made the decisions, he's the strategist and helps me work out the bigger plan and how things are going to work on the ground.*'

'*It's not really consciously there in my mind any more in the way it was when I was younger,*' reflects Adam. '*I know what I want to get done and find a way to achieve that, but it hasn't always been easy. One of the biggest challenges of running a business is that you have to get out there and market yourself which means speaking to lots of different people, and that hasn't always been easy.'* Adam talks about how with his business partner he has moved out of his comfort zone by challenging him to new ways of working without much preparation. Adam now regularly makes presentations such as speaking at the MADE Festival for Entrepreneurs in 2011, and participating in the National Council for Voluntary Youth Services with youth parliament activities.

'Aspergers comes second now,' says Adam. *'Others with the same condition can learn what I've done but it takes practice and confidence. I spend quite a lot of time analysing what I'm doing in the third person as well as talking with friends in my personal network.'*

WHAT ADVICE WOULD YOU GIVE TO YOUNG PEOPLE NOW IF THEY WANT TO BE MORE ENTERPRISING?

'Be creative', whatever age you are, even if you're 16 go and do some art, just do something creative.

'Make sure you have family time, it's easy when you grow up to spend more and more time with friends from school, but it's so important to keep that rapport with your family too. Family time is important, not just in terms of doing enterprising activities together but just being together, a walk in the park, a meal, simple things'.

'Keep an open mind, think beyond just what you see and hear, and keep learning.'

And for parents, Adam also has a message. *'Don't forget what it's like to be a child yourself,'* he smiles.

You can find out more about Adam's business activities at www.unitecomputing.com

LUKE COUSINS aged 22 founded *VioVet* – the online pet food and medication business when he was still at school. *VioVet* is a family run business and six years on has sales expected to exceed £10m in the current financial year.

A separate interview with Luke's parents John and Sharon is available to read on the Enterprising Child website.

HOW DO YOU THINK YOUR PARENTS PLAYED A ROLE IN YOU BECOMING AN ENTREPRENEUR?

They certainly did not sit me down to try and drum things into me, but they always encouraged me. Obviously while I was growing up, I saw them running their own business, so that would have definitely influenced me.

I think the first time I thought seriously about earning money, was when Dad brought home someone's pet budgerigar to look after. I got £10 for that. It was such a great way to earn some money, so in the end I started looking after loads of pets.

After that, I started buying and selling things on eBay. Once, I bought a big job lot and then sold items off, one by one. I didn't earn much, but I enjoyed the experience. I was doing my GCSEs at the time. My parents encouraged me to focus on my studies, so in the end, I sold everything so that I could focus on my GCSEs. Of course, after I finished my GCSEs I started to think, 'Right, now what else can I do!'

YOU STARTED VIOVET WHEN YOU WERE STILL AT SCHOOL. WHAT WERE THE CHALLENGES IN RUNNING A BUSINESS WHILE STILL AT SCHOOL?

There were lots of challenges. My teachers couldn't grasp the concept that I was running a real business. On the odd occasion that I was late

— and trust me, it was very rare — perhaps due to a rush order on the website or something like that, some teachers just didn't believe me. Of course, some teachers were very supportive. No-one at school tried to stop me, but I think they probably couldn't accept that running a business was a better use of my time than studying for A levels.

It's a very good private school, and practically everyone who goes there, goes on to university. I mean a good university. They used to have career evenings where they would invite a business leader to talk to the students about career aspirations. At the time, they didn't think of inviting in an entrepreneur. But I have since been invited back to talk to the students myself and I understand that they do have entrepreneur evenings now.

My other challenge was that I was so young and the vast majority of our staff was at least 10 years older than me. That was challenging, trying to tell people what to do. It was really helpful having my parents there to support me. In fact, very often, I would make the decision, and my parents would convey it to the staff — especially if it was over something that was a bit awkward, my parents could be far more diplomatic than I could.

In fact, there's no way I would have been able to run this business without my parents there to support me. When the business was first up and running, we only had a desk in the corner of the room. Everything had to be run from that one desk — accounts, PAYE, etc. Well these were things that I had absolutely no idea about. I couldn't have done that myself. They provided the base for me to build the business on.

DO YOU HAVE ANY TIPS FOR OTHER YOUNGSTERS WHO ARE THINKING ABOUT STARTING UP A BUSINESS?
I've spoken to lots of friends who think they can't start a business because they have no money. I started VioVet with only £200 — and that was from my parents! So, you don't need thousands of pounds.

But I would suggest go to your parents for advice. My parents were really supportive, we talk about everything. As I said before, there's no way I could have done this without their support.

My other advice is to be realistic. It's hard to be realistic when you're young, you easily get carried away. Finish your studies and run the business in the evenings and weekends. Scale up when your studies are over. I would have preferred to leave school and run the business full-time, but it was my mum who said, 'No, focus on your A Levels. Don't burn your bridges.' In hindsight, I think she was right. If I had left to run the business full-time and the business failed, then I would have had nothing to fall back on. But now, if at some point I do decide to do something else, at least I have my A levels and they're good grades, so I could go on to do something else if I really wanted to.

I would also say embrace technology. The internet is the future, so use it to your advantage. Learn as much as you can about modern technology. It's not hard. I built my website myself.

Otherwise, go for it. Nothing ventured, nothing gained. You can do anything if you're really motivated to do it.

AS A YOUNG ENTREPRENEUR, WHAT WOULD BE YOUR ADVICE TO PARENTS?
Obviously this isn't something you can force someone to do. If your child really isn't interested, then fine. But if they are showing signs of wanting to work for themselves then I would say definitely be supportive.

Don't just readily dole out loads of money. I think if I had a son and he wanted to start a business, I would want him to write a business plan and then I would oversee it – more so that he doesn't get conned.

AND FINALLY, CAN YOU SEE YOURSELF EVER BEING AN EMPLOYEE?
I love the flexibility of being able to work the hours that I want to work. Sometimes it's a long day, other times it's not. I can go on holiday whenever I want to. So no, I don't think so!

EMILY CUMMINS is an inventor who is passionate about sustainable designs that change lives. Her inventions include a sustainable fridge powered by dirty water, an adaptable water carrier for use in third world countries where long journeys are necessary to collect water, and a toothpaste dispenser to help people who have conditions affecting their hands such as arthritis.

Emily has received a host of awards for her inventions and actions, not least the 2010 JCI Ten Outstanding Young Persons of the World Award, the 2008 Future 100 Young Entrepreneur of the Year, and 2007 Female Innovator of the Year.

Emily is 25 years old.

TELL US A LITTLE ABOUT YOUR CHILDHOOD AND YOUR PARENTS
'My mum has a senior position in the pharmaceutical industry. She is a very driven person and has always worked hard to succeed. After a long day at work, she would come home and start on the house, the cleaning and cooking, she never stopped,' explains Emily. Her father was a fireman and although he didn't have the same drive for promotion as her mum, he was very much into health and wellbeing, regularly visiting the gym.

'My grandparents and cousins lived locally, so as a child, I spent a lot of my time with them. My brother was born when I was 3½ years old and I was the eldest of the grandchildren.'

ARE THERE ANY PARTICULAR MEMORIES YOU HAVE FROM WHEN YOU WERE A CHILD WHICH WERE THE KEY TO UNLOCKING THE INTEREST YOU DEVELOPED IN DESIGN AND INNOVATION?
'Definitely. The highlight of going to my grandparents was spending time in Grandad's shed where, from the age of four, I had my own

hammer to help him with making and fixing things. He would often make furniture for Mum, so I would watch or help where I could. Being the eldest meant I could spend more time there than the others and my granddad would often ask me what toys I wanted to make from scrap materials in his shed. At such a young age I was able to experiment and explore; he ignited my creative spark which is something I will always carry with me.'

Emily goes on to explain that throughout her primary years, whilst spending time with her granddad, she learned to make items such as jewellery boxes, rabbit hutches and toy trucks and had the skills to use the sander, pillar drill and the lathe. Her mum was fairly handy around the house, too, changing fuses, wiring TV aerials and fixing broken toys, so Emily's introduction to inventing and fixing things came very much from around close family members. Her parents' attitude towards her education was to 'try hard', although she refused to go to an all girls grammar school, preferring instead to follow the crowd and go to a state secondary.

When starting secondary school, her dad gave her an incentive to do well. *'He told me for every merit I achieved at school, he would give me £1 and at the end of the academic year, if I got more than any other student he would double the amount. It was a great incentive for me; I received the most merits in my year group for four years running and became one of the top achievers across the board.'* Interestingly, her brother was offered the same incentive but didn't really try for the merits. *'We had different outlooks on money, though. I was always a saver and appreciated the value of money; my brother was much more flippant. I have to work hard at everything,'* says Emily, *'and if I'm doing well then I really go for it. The flip side of that, though, is if I'm struggling and not doing my best then I get disheartened and often need a kick to stop giving up.'*

'By the time I arrived at secondary school I was considered to be a
handy person, creating and mending things as required, but the fact
is, that just isn't cool when you're a teenager and I didn't feel happy
sharing what I did with others, so I gradually spent less and less time
over at Granddad's.'

Emily took an interest in sports, encouraged by her dad, and
started to lose interest in making things. Technology was
introduced at school, but it was 'disappointingly so basic, we had to
all make the same products, how uncreative is that! As a child, I could
make whatever I wanted, so didn't like being told what we had to
design and make,' so although she was able to use her skills to help
classmates out, she felt very frustrated by it all.

Did she not tell the teachers about her abilities? 'No, I didn't want
to single myself out. Resistant Materials (Design &Technology) was
considered a boys' subject and, in my peers' eyes, girls weren't
expected to be interested. Thinking back now, I can't understand why
students weren't being taught how to use equipment and then given
the opportunity to create their own products, this is what my
granddad did with me and it certainly inspired my creativity! No
wonder we lose the interest of so many young people during their
secondary school years.'

Although Emily's spark for technology was dampened, she tried
really hard at school across all subjects and when it came to
choosing her GCSE options she had to choose a technology based
subject and selected Product Design, 'simply because all my friends
had chosen it'. However, she didn't get that first choice and was put
into a Resistant Materials class instead with 17 boys and only one
other girl! Upon reaching the classroom, suddenly, a spark of

interest had been re-ignited. *'It was like being back in Grandad's shed;'* smiles Emily, *'the class was held in an old building at the back of the school which I'd never been to before. We had a great teacher whose style reminded me of my granddad, and we were encouraged to experiment and design and make our own products.'* From this free rein, Emily decided to make something of real value and remembered how her other granddad was struggling with arthritis in his hands. Inspired by this, she made her first product, the toothpaste dispenser, which was then entered into a competition by the school. *'I was shy, and didn't expect to win,'* says Emily. *'I had to present in front of a panel of judges and the thought was daunting. In school I was the kind of person to stand at the front of a class holding a poster over my face. However, when the judges criticised my design, my passion shone through and I found a voice that day (that I have never lost) that enabled me to stand up for my design. This voice helped me win, and I couldn't believe it.'*

After winning the competition, Emily went on to study for her A Level in Product Design, and her teacher offered her the opportunity to work on the Sustainable Design Award through which she built the water carrier, then in her second year went on to design her sustainable refrigerator. This fridge is now used across Southern Africa, produced by women and improving the quality of both the lives of the women who are creating them and the people who are able to use them. This required a considerable amount of research, *'but when I realised I could help people with my products, they became even more important and I wanted them to be the very best they possibly could.'*

REFLECTING ON ALL THAT HAS HAPPENED SO FAR, WHO WOULD YOU SAY HAS INFLUENCED YOU THE MOST?
'My granddad ignited the spark of creativity and innovation within me, there's no question about that, but Mum's drive and passion to

do well have also played a huge part in my life. She has never been a pushy mum in any way, but has modelled the behaviour and attitudes she wanted me to learn.'

WHAT ADVICE WOULD YOU GIVE TO PARENTS READING THIS BOOK?
'Let your child explore and take a bit of risk, let them try lots of different things to find out what they really enjoy'.

'It's important for you to model the behaviour of how you want your child to be, my mum is very driven and worked incredibly hard, but I never felt pressure to be this way, I just learned from what she showed me that working hard can bring positive results.'

AND WHAT WOULD YOU SAY TO YOUNG PEOPLE WHO WANT TO BECOME MORE ENTERPRISING?
'Try to stand out from the crowd from as young an age as possible, don't just follow everyone else. I missed out on loads of opportunities because I thought it wasn't cool to speak up'.

'Use the time and resources at school well, and try lots of different things to discover what your passion is.'

You can visit Emily's web site and see her inventions at www.emilycummins.co.uk

JAMIE DUNN is an entrepreneur, international speaker, newspaper columnist, mentor, and Youth Excellence award winner. As if that wasn't enough, he is also Chair of *The A Fund* – a £10 million investment fund set up for young people in Birmingham to develop enterprises.

Prior to joining *The A Fund*, Jamie co-founded and was Managing Director of *Made by Young People*, a print company creating enterprise and employment opportunities for young people and running enterprise workshops in schools and colleges.

Jamie started his first business aged just 12. He is now 20 years old.

TELL US A LITTLE ABOUT YOUR CHILDHOOD AND WHAT YOUR FAMILY DID FOR A LIVING.

I grew up in a suburb of Birmingham called Erdington, not far from Kingstanding, which has one of the highest crime and unemployment rates in the UK. My older two (half) brothers both work (one is now very senior in the police, the other a recruitment consultant), but my older two (half) sisters are both unemployed, looking after their families, one of whom is a single mum with three children.

My dad and mum have been together 20 years. Mum used to work in a residential home for the elderly but has remained unemployed since being made redundant from there. Dad worked for years as a manual labourer with the local council until at the age of 50 (I was 11), when he had to be moved to another job due to becoming partially deaf from all the work he did on the roads. He spent the last 10 years as a union representative, and really enjoyed it.'

Jamie goes on to explain that he wasn't really interested in academia; he found it '*boring and tedious. As my brothers had done well for themselves, the general feeling at home was, well your brothers did fine so you'll be fine too. My parents didn't really push me to do anything,'* he explains.

When it comes to work ethic, Jamie is clear that that precedent was set by his dad with an army background and then manual labouring out on the roads, working all hours. *'Mum worked hard too, though,'* said Jamie, *'she brought up five children, cooked, cleaned and ran the house.'*

ARE THERE ANY PARTICULAR MEMORIES YOU HAVE WHICH YOU FEEL INFLUENCED DECISIONS YOU WENT ON TO MAKE ABOUT EDUCATION OR WORK?

'Definitely' says Jamie. *'I remember well how every Christmas I never saw Dad. He was always working extra shifts, taking every bit of work he could to make our Christmas's special so there were lots of presents around the tree.'* One Christmas, however, his father was too ill to work and consequently there was just one present each. Jamie was 11 at the time, fast approaching his 12th birthday in the January, and clearly remembers asking his dad *'What's happened? Dad took me to one side and said now I was a teenager I needed to understand things better. He told me I shouldn't end up where he was, breaking his back to put food on the table. He said I was smart, I should do well and that I should be happy.'*

That proved to be a turning point for Jamie who, by the time his 12th birthday arrived the following month, had decided he didn't want to have to struggle through life working hard for little money.

SO WHAT HAPPENED NEXT AND HOW DID YOU GET INTO STARTING YOUR OWN BUSINESS SO YOUNG?

'I was due to start secondary school. I really didn't want to go', says Jamie, *'but I also knew that I had to do something to start making money.'* By the end of the first few weeks at school, Jamie had

tipped out his bag of school books and started to fill it with his parents' CD collection. *'I took them in to school and started flogging them to the teachers. The first day I made £60,'* he smiles.

Didn't his parents mind? *'Well, they weren't too happy,'* replies Jamie, *'they took the money off me that I'd made to pay for replacement CDs.'* And the school's response? *'They called my parents in and said I shouldn't do it again. They said I wasn't focused enough at school, and that I had to try harder.'*

This was a second turning point for Jamie. He realised what interested him and decided right then that he would begin his business career. Starting with car boot sales, Jamie helped out his dad, who often went to one at weekends. *'The problem was,'* said Jamie, *'Dad was only paying me £10 even though I worked all day. I didn't want someone paying me in that way, so we negotiated that I would help out more, do more regular boot sales and take a bigger share of money earned'.* From there, Jamie visited friends and collected as many items as possible to sell on. He learned to agree a price with them beforehand. *'It taught me so many things,'* he said, *'not least about waking up in the mornings, and taking responsibility.'*

Still going to school, Jamie enlisted support from his unemployed sisters to help out with sourcing goods from wholesalers for his stall. He started to focus on items which sold well such as CDs and DVDs, and by the age of 15 was earning between £300 profit on a bad day to £600 profit on a good one. *'Getting my sisters involved was important because I learned then that I didn't need to work too hard to earn money, I could get others to do that for me.'*

SO THE BUSINESS PATHWAY WAS ALL MAPPED OUT FOR YOU THEN? *'Not exactly. The thing is, I was actually playing football from an early age and by the time I reached 15 I was playing for the Birmingham Academy four or five times a week.'* Jamie's parents believed he was going to be a footballer and therefore didn't really need to worry about succeeding at basic subjects such as English and Maths at school. Jamie believed that too and didn't really try too hard, until an incident on the field halted what might have been a glittering career. *'It was a horrible time,'* Jamie reflects. *'I had a stud go through my kneecap out on the field. I ended up having reconstructive surgery on my knee and the end result was I just couldn't play to the standard I needed to, so the trainee place planned for me at 16 was offered to someone else.'*

This incident set Jamie right back. He realised he was no longer going to be a footballer and became depressed. He lost motivation and stopped everything, including all the market stalls that were doing so well. *'It hit my dad too,'* said Jamie sadly. *'It was his dream as well; he had never been good enough to go professional and my brother had turned the opportunity down previously.'* Everyone was asking Jamie what he was going to do next and he didn't know.

Around July, when the GCSE results were due out, Jamie realised that all his friends were planning their futures, many going into college. *'I guess I just followed them and thought I might as well go to College too. Once I'd got my results – they weren't good – I applied to study Business, Law, English Literature, and History.'* It wasn't easy to get on the course and Jamie explained how he had to plead with his Business Studies tutor to accept him. Within a short time of being on the course, and just before Christmas again, another significant event happened. His parents happened to mention a programme they'd been watching about the millionaire businessman Peter Jones and how he was looking for young people to apply to his National Enterprise Academy Pathfinder programme. *'I applied, but I honestly didn't expect to get in,'* said Jamie. *'I'd lost a lot of confidence and although I didn't find the college classes very challenging, I was settled there.'* Jamie's parents were supportive of his application, once they'd checked that he was really sure he wanted to do it, which was just as well as in the middle of a college business class Jamie received the call to say he had been shortlisted for an assessment day at the Academy.

His dad had to borrow the money to get them all to the assessment centre and he recalls them turning up in a rusty old Ford and parking up next to a Bentley and a Ferrari. *'I felt nervous, really nervous,'* said Jamie. *'I didn't own a suit, and I remember saying to Dad how scared I was.'* The other applicants were older than Jamie, all wearing suits, and he pleaded with his dad to take him back home. *'Dad wasn't having any of it. He said, "Look, Son, regardless of what they do and how they look, they're just a human being like you."* That was all it took for Jamie to walk through the doors, pass the assessment, and six months later, after a move to Buckinghamshire to complete the course, graduate with flying colours. The rest, as they say, is history, and Jamie has already packed a lot into a few short years since leaving the Academy.

WHAT DO YOUR PARENTS THINK OF WHAT YOU'VE ACHIEVED SO FAR?
'They're so supportive,' smiles Jamie. *'Mum is quite hands off, she just thinks I should go with whatever I feel is right, but Dad and I meet up regularly to go to football or to the pub. We'll talk about how things are going and if I ever start to feel down about something that isn't working or that I don't feel I'm doing well at, he reminds me of what I have done, what I have achieved.'*

WHAT ADVICE WOULD YOU GIVE TO PARENTS READING THIS BOOK?
'Give your children the freedom to explore and make mistakes. I was allowed to have independence from an early age and that was a strong factor in what I'm doing now. It's easy to forget that you were once a child, so try to remember when you were their age and don't get angry with them.'

'Be there to support them and help them learn. Don't have expectations, just make sure they're happy.'

'*Don't do things just to please your parents,*' says Jamie with a smile. '*It's fine to be a bit selfish — why please others if you're not going to be happy yourself?*' This is one of the key reasons Jamie believes children become angry and foster resentment. '*I'm not saying be disrespectful, just to know your own mind, talk to your parents, explore your options.*'

'*And remember,*' he says finally, '*regardless of what you're doing now, you don't have to be doing that forever.*'

You can visit Jamie's web site at **www.jamie-dunn.com**

JAMES HEADSPEATH is a 24 year old student at Southampton Solent University, runs his own business and is a twice successful Ironman triathlete. In early 2012 he was named 'one of the most employable young people in the UK' by *Google* and *Entrepreneur Country*.

That in itself sounds pretty impressive, but when you add in the fact that in 2008 he'd dropped out of university, was unemployed and then diagnosed with chronic urticaria - a serious and rare medical condition meaning he was essentially allergic to exercise, you begin to realise there is more to James than first meets the eye, and a story to tell which will inspire both parents and young people alike.

TELL US A LITTLE ABOUT YOUR CHILDHOOD AND THE KIND OF VALUES YOUR PARENTS INSTILLED IN YOU.

'I was born in England, but spent from age three to six living in Washington DC,' explains James. *'My mother was a teacher and my father a government worker. I guess you could say it was a fairly comfortable upbringing, we did a lot of travelling and there seemed to be no worries about anything. Having said that I didn't have any leg up in the world – my parents' view was always if you want to succeed and live a comfortable life then you have to work hard, achieve academically, and secure a good job.'*

James goes on to explain that in many ways he felt his childhood was lived in a bubble, even back in the UK, and has no memories of ever really having any worries. *'I didn't even feel I could really identify with the average lifestyle of being a young person,'* says James, *'I just sat back and relaxed, I just didn't know the world was any different.'*

Whilst his parents' work ethics were strong, James did find the focus on academia difficult. *'Throughout school I didn't really work very hard. It wasn't that I was lazy, I just saw school as a kind of necessary evil.'* Weren't his parents worried about his laid back approach to studies? *'They were very supportive,'* says James. *'Yes, they did believe that hard work, including academic studies, would bring me success, I think they also recognised that I wasn't particularly interested in or even very good at academic studies.'* James recalls his mother often saying to him 'Everything will work out in the end.'

SO WHAT WAS THE TURNING POINT WHICH MADE YOU REALISE THERE WAS MORE THAN ONE WORLD OUT THERE?

'I managed to get through my A levels with just three at E grade and 1 at U grade. The turning point was after I left university.' James was studying business and management but realised after just two months that more studying wasn't for him, but he stuck it out for a year, then left. At that point he had no job, no decent qualifications, and didn't really know what he wanted to do. *'I had this sense that, although my parents had taught me that working hard and academic achievements would lead to success, actually in large part natural talent was also a requirement and I didn't see that I had any of that either.'* He goes on to mention that his brother, who was not only good at sports but also academia, seemed more of a natural than him in all aspects.

HOW DID YOU GET INTO SPORT AND WHAT HAPPENED WHEN YOU WERE DIAGNOSED WITH CHRONIC URTICARIA?

'Well, although I wasn't a naturally good sports person (often being the last to be picked on school teams), I found enjoyment in sport when I was at university, mainly because in my mind there was nothing else to do. I wasn't interested in the academic side of things so I joined the gym and started running.' James goes on to explain that his involvement in sport became almost obsessive, but something happened when he was playing rugby which gave him quite a scare

– on several occasions his whole body appeared to swell, leaving him short of breath. *'I didn't know what was going on; it was happening about once a month and becoming more frequent and bizarrely seemed to be every time I played sport, it was quite scary.'*

In 2008 James was referred to a doctor who, after various tests, announced that he had a potentially life threatening and rare condition called chronic urticaria which basically meant he was allergic to exercise. *'The doctor was very pessimistic,'* he reflects. *'He prescribed medication, but said the results and successes with it were variable, and under no circumstances was I to participate in any kind of intensive sport.'*

Having left university and with no job in the pipeline, watching his friends going in to successful jobs and with a diagnosis meaning he couldn't participate in the one thing that he most enjoyed, James explains how he found himself in a very difficult and dark place. *'It would have been easy to feel very low. It was my first real adversity and it had the potential to make me or break me.'* For a while he did as the doctor suggested and exchanged playing sport for watching films and video. However, the Ironman videos he watched sparked a particular interest. To begin with he watched them just for enjoyment, but then he came across two videos which had a real impact. *'I've loved American football since I was young,'* explained James, *'and I came across a video about Tom Brady* (for anyone not familiar, Tom Brady is an American football quarterback and considered to be one of America's finest athletes). *'It was interesting to read his struggle to succeed as although he was a good athlete in school, when it came to professional sport his abilities were questioned, for example he was considered too small for playing at that level, not strong enough, too skinny, but he went on to prove them wrong.'*

James sensed similarities to his own situation. The second video he watched was of a man with two prosthetic legs completing the

Ironman. *'That was it,'* said James. *'I told myself I was going to do it.'* So he went against the doctor's advice and, despite not being about to swim (he watched a video on how to swim[87]) or run and cycle very far, he entered the race. His only recollection of his parents' reaction to this huge decision was them checking whether he was absolutely sure about it. *'Their response was, well if you think it's the right thing to do, then we'll support you,'* says James.

'It was through the first adversity that I decided something had to change, that I should really try again at academia and give it my very best shot.' It wasn't to be that simple, however, as James's first five universities of choice rejected him outright with such poor A level results. He then applied to another four universities until eventually the ninth (Solent) accepted him. *'I can't help but wonder, if I had been accepted by the first university I applied to, whether things would be different now, but the fact is I'm here now and enjoying what I do.'*

When he finally returned to university in 2009, James was still suffering from the chronic urticaria, but had a different mental attitude. *'I knew I had to work hard and I'd promised myself that I wouldn't lose the second opportunity I'd been given,'* said James. He signed up to a triathlete club but found he couldn't even swim two lengths of the pool. Determined to prove others wrong and complete the Ironman contest, he worked hard not just at his studies but at becoming fitter. In July 2010 he entered his very first Ironman in Belgium and completed the course. Interestingly, he had no medical emergencies and got through the course without problems. *'When it was over I remember saying to my parents that I was going to do it again. They asked me if I was sure, I think they were*

[87]swimsmooth.com

266

concerned about putting my body back through something like that again, but I knew it was something I had to do.' In 2011, James successfully completed his second Ironman competition and was also offered a sports scholarship at the Solent University Athletic Network Development for Triathlon and Cycling.

SO, HOW DID YOU GET INTO RUNNING YOUR OWN BUSINESS?

'It was after completing the second Ironman when I felt I just had more mental strength,' says James. 'There was an inter-university business competition taking place in Nottingham which caught my eye, but I realised that at my university we didn't even have a business club, so I decided to set one up.' This was a second turning point for James when he realised his interest in business and decided to start his own (iChallengeU).

'My parents have stayed completely out of the business,' says James. 'They expressed some concern about the risks involved, but I told them to let me worry about that! It doesn't even feel like risk.' James explains that the company is going through a re-branding process at the moment and that he has successfully secured external investment so that when he leaves university (with a BA Hons Marketing with Advertising Management) in Summer 2012 he will be walking straight into his own office space. 'It feels great. I don't feel any pressure in the way I did when I was at school or university and it just feels like the most natural thing to be doing.'

In reflecting on past events James is very pragmatic and recognises that things could have been quite different, and not just in terms of going back to university or fighting against the illness. The biggest issue for him was breaking the myth that only natural talent will bring success. 'Had I understood that there was really no such thing as natural talent much earlier then things might have been quite different for me,' he reflects, going on to comment that actually anything can be achieved with, as he describes it, *'sickeningly hard work'.* He continues, with a broad smile, *'But I'm glad about everything that's happened, from the diagnosis and dropping out of university to being rejected by all those universities in my attempt to study again, as through those adversities I am where I am today.'*

WHAT ADVICE WOULD YOU GIVE TO YOUNG PEOPLE NOW IF THEY WANT TO BECOME MORE ENTERPRISING?
'Whatever your goal is, believe you can do it and don't be afraid to fail. I don't care if I fail,' he explains. *'Obviously I never aim to fail and I always aim to win in everything I do, but if I do fail then I take all the positives I can from it, although I'm still annoyed!*

'Failure should never be viewed as a negative. There is a perception that naturally talented people don't fail – this is simply not true. Everyone fails at some point; it's how you deal with it that matters. For me, I want to do something even more if I fail – failure motivates me to learn more and succeed.'

Watch James in action at the Global Entrepreneurship Week[88]

---

[88]http://www.youtube.com/watch?v=2_mQPMfWDNU&feature=related

JENNIFER OKPAPI is founder of *Akhaya Cookery School.* Jennifer managed to turn her passion for food into the UK's first cookery school dedicated to African cuisine which now offers a range of day classes and courses as well as its own range of food products.

TELL US ABOUT YOUR BACKGROUND AND HOW YOU FEEL YOUR PARENTS NURTURED A GOOD WORK ETHIC IN YOU.

At university I studied Business Management and Computing. However, I have always loved cooking. My parents encouraged me to experiment from a young age and I was often encouraged to cook for family meal times. I think I probably fell in love with the food of our Nigerian culture first. I have always been fascinated with spices and bringing beautiful flavours together. I set up the business in 2010 after studying professional cookery at college.

My parents have always encouraged us to aim high, especially in school, and have always encouraged us to be the very best we can be. In many respects they had an entrepreneurial mindset themselves as they always worked and were always trying their hand at different things.

HAVE YOU HAD ANY CHALLENGES IN RUNNING YOUR BUSINESS? WHAT LESSONS HAVE YOU LEARNED?

I would say that the most challenging aspect was starting it and getting it up and running. Otherwise, the other challenges were obtaining funding. Overall, it was challenging, but not daunting.

I think in business you need to be very determined. It is important to hold your own, and not be discouraged by others who think you can't do it, or who think you won't succeed.

Running your own business is definitely not an easy route to take, even with the rise of enterprise in the U.K. So I would say be aware of the challenges that you could potentially face.

WHAT ADVICE WOULD YOU GIVE TO OTHER PARENTS, WHO ARE KEEN TO NURTURE THE ENTREPRENEURIAL POTENTIAL IN THEIR CHILDREN?
I would say that if you as a parent run a business yourself, talk about your business with your child. Try and involve your children if and where you can. Talk about what you do and how you do it to provide an introduction to business for your children.

Otherwise, I would say to try and recognise your child's passion. Find out what it is they love doing, and nurture it.

Epilogue

This book was written knowing that developing children's entrepreneurial potential was important, both for their own future success and for the benefit of the wider community. Though many parents are doing their best to help support their child's creativity and zest for life, there seems to be a general lack of focus on the role and significance of parents in developing children's entrepreneurial potential.

The stories told here by successful entrepreneurs and business leaders about their parents' influence in their own childhood, and by parents sharing their experiences of helping their children make the best of themselves and create their own possibilities, have been both informative and inspirational.

All our children are busy writing the stories of their own lives and as parents we are there in the very centre of that story, helping to shape its outcome by all that we do and say. I hope you have found this book helpful in making sense of your own contribution to your child's story.

Thank you so much for taking the time to read it, and, whatever else you think about the opinions or guidance offered, we are certainly united in the desire to help our children to be the best that they can be.

This book has been written as a beginning not as an end so, as well as hoping you have found some inspiration and practical help, I hope you will join us as we continue to learn from each other, and from our children, about the best ways to help them realise their potential.

The Enterprising Child web site and online community has been developed to accompany this book and I hope you will feel inspired to explore the resources it offers and to contribute your own experiences and ideas.

Whatever happens, do continue to enjoy the journey you are taking with your enterprising child, and may it continue to be a source of joy, wonder and fun, for you and for them.

Enterprising Child web site – access all areas

The Enterprising Child web site has been designed to support readers of this book, in particular parents, who are interested in developing the entrepreneurial potential in children aged 4 to 14 years old. It is a comprehensive and interactive resource, encouraging the sharing of experiences and ideas and providing regular features and comments on subjects related to the development of children's entrepreneurial potential.

There is an area of the site dedicated exclusively to purchasers of this book which you can access by scanning the QR code or entering the web site address below. You then gain access to further resources, including downloads, videos, and a discussion forum as well as additional interviews carried out during the research for, and the writing of, this book.

Visit **www.enterprisingchild.com/booksignup.php?id=e7948** now, or scan the QR code to access all areas.

 Lorraine Allman is a mum, business woman, researcher, and mentor with over 12 years' experience running businesses, and supporting adults and young people, to do the same. She started her working life providing personal development courses for young people then after a successful management career in Higher Education moved on to work freelance supporting an arts education initiative designed to encourage school children to 'Opt for Art'. From there she was involved in a second arts education project 'SchoolArt'.

In the late 1990's Lorraine established one of the first online business information portals in the UK and went on to run several other companies including a business and educational research company focused on social enterprises, adult and community learning in the Third sector, and researching levels of participation among young people in public decision making.

As well as now running Speed Mentor Central, Lorraine mentors business start-ups and is a Band Leader of the Community Interest Company *Enterprise Rockers*.

Lorraine lives in West Wales with her husband and six year old son.

Mary Cummings is an entrepreneur and freelance writer, who established her first business in 2005 as a Virtual Assistant supporting small businesses in South East and Central London. After experiencing the challenges of starting a business with young children in tow, she now runs an established and successful online community called Work Your Way™ providing small business resources for Freelance and Self-Employed mums. Mary lives in South East London with her husband and three children.

Lightning Source UK Ltd.
Milton Keynes UK
UKOW07f1404160115

244588UK00005B/86/P